Determine Your Own Future, or Someone Else Will

The Seven-Step Guide to Plan for Self Determination

Marcelene Anderson

DETERMINE YOUR OWN FUTURE, OR SOMEONE ELSE WILL
THE SEVEN-STEP GUIDE TO PLAN FOR SELF DETERMINATION

iUniverse books may be ordered through booksellers or by contacting:

iUniverse
1663 Liberty Drive
Bloomington, IN 47403
www.iuniverse.com
844-349-9409

ISBN: 978-1-6632-1819-3 (sc)
ISBN: 978-1-6632-1821-6 (hc)
ISBN: 978-1-6632-1820-9 (e)

Library of Congress Control Number: 2021923712

Print information available on the last page.

iUniverse rev. date: 11/14/2022

*We better pay attention to
the future because that is
where we are going to spend
the rest of our lives there.*

Joe Barker

About This Book

The title of this book has a two-part name: *Determine Your Future, or Someone Else Will*. Although *Determine Your Future* could apply to personal planning, it is, in fact, about organizational planning. More specifically, this book is dedicated to planning for native peoples in the Americas and worldwide, in Canada called Indigenous People. "Determining" implies making decisions, being proactive, taking charge of one's future. Claiming to decide your future is a powerful self-declaration that I am responsible for my future. I am in charge. For millieums, Native and Indigenous Peoples had determined their future.

The second part of the title *or, Someone Else Will*, is significant. For centuries Indigenous and Native Peoples have been denied the right to make their own decisions. It may be difficult for non-Indigenous or non-Natives to understand why and how this came to be. The origins of the Doctrine of Discovery were not taught in public schools across North America but have had far devastating, profound implications that continue to this day.

Sadly, not one non-Indigenous person I have spoken with was familiar with the Doctrine of Discovery. Not one. Nor were several persons of Indigenous heritage, I asked. They are shocked when they are informed and immediately understand the vast consequences of it. At the recent Pope's apology visit to Canada, Indigenous people across Canada continue to call for the Doctrine of Discovery to be rescinded, now with a stronger voice, while increasing the awareness of it with all Canadians and the necessity of addressing this issue.

The Doctrine of Discovery is a set of man-made rules that became accepted as legitimate for the purpose and convenience of the land hungry who wanted to expand their territory and gain resources. It disregarded and nullified the existence of Indigenous Peoples who had occupied their territories since time immemorial because they did not follow the Christian faith.

The Doctrine of Discovery, which originated as far back as 1493, became the international law, giving license to explorers to claim vacant land (terra nullius) in the name of their sovereign. That is, vacant land not populated by Christians. The occupants were not regarded as human, based on the Papal Bull, Doctrine of Discovery, 1493.[1]

Briefly, it states. "If Christians did not occupy the land, they were considered vacant, therefore could be defined as "discovered," allowing sovereignty, dominion, title, and jurisdiction claimed. It gave sovereignty or title of Indigenous traditional lands and territories to the Crown."[2] It remains today "the legal justification for the colonial occupation of lands and nations."

Although some thought the land in North America was unoccupied, it was far from vacant when European explorers

---

[1] Ronald Wright, *Stolen Continents: The "New World" Through Indian Eyes*, (1999) p 4

[2] Robert J. Miller, <u>The Doctrine of Discovery: The International Law of Colonialism</u>

began arriving. When Christopher Columbus arrived in 1492, 100 million Indigenous Peoples who constituted one-fifth of the world's population, occupied the lands.[3] But, since they were not Christians, they were not considered humans and the land vacant.

Indigenous Peoples in Canada have waged multiple, lengthy legal battles to prove their existence before the arrival of European explorers. The Doctrine of Discovery is important today because it has never been renounced and remains the basis for Canadian law, and therefore continues to impact Indigenous Peoples to this day.[4]

It made possible the Indian Act and its genocidal laws and policies, such as the residential school system and removal of Indigenous Peoples from traditional lands to reserves, criminalization of languages and cultural ceremonies, creation, recognition, and later denial of Treaty and Indigenous rights.[5]

Increasingly, Native and Indigenous Peoples have fought for their rights and recognition, and often court decisions favouring Native rights are appealed or challenged by governments or the Crown.

It is time for new rules to be created and recognized. Ones that respect the rights of all people. This may sound like utopia. New world orders come into existence by people willing to dream and challenge the status quo.

---

[3] Arthur Manuel and Grand Chief Ron Derrickson. Between the Lines, *Unsettling Canada A National Wake-Up Call*, p 10
[4] Sylvia McAdam, author of Dismantling the Doctrine of Discovery: A Call to Action, Wrong to Right, Common Word
[5] Robert J. Miller, The Doctrine of Discovery: The International Law of Colonialism

The Assembly of First Nation report on Dismantling the Doctrine of Discover 2018 states it is essential to ensure a paradigm that is truthful about the history of past relations between First Nations and settlers be told. Everyone must recognize that Indigenous Peoples in sovereign nations occupied the land before contact.[6]

The time is always right to do right.

Dr. Martin Luther King Jr.

Sylvia McAdam, author of Dismantling the Doctrine of Discovery: A Call to Action, says the power resides in each of us to seek recourse when we see injustice. The Doctrine of Discovery effects all of us. If you are against the domination and discrimination of any peoples, then seek to question the information provided here and, together, let us do something so that a wrong can be corrected.[7]

The second part of the title of this book *or, Someone Else Will* recognizes the importance of Native and Indigenous Peoples making decisions for themselves and their future. Long before Europeans arrived in the Americas, Native People had been self-governing.

The phrase "or Someone Else Will" originated by the late GE CEO, Jack Welsh, who, revealing a universal truth, said, "Control your destiny or someone else will."

Many factors influence our ability to control our destiny,

---

[6] Assembly of First Nations | Dismantling the Doctrine of Discovery | January 2018
[7] Sylvia McAdam, author of Dismantling the Doctrine of Discovery: A Call to Action, Wrong to Right, Common Word

ranging from weather, inflation, the economy, government regulations, and a multitude of factors. However, we are not helpless. We can make choices for ourselves, our families, organizations, communities, and nations.

We have a God, Creator-given right to make decisions for our lives and future.

This book intends to provide you with a proven process to determine the future of your organization, community, or nation, thereby clarifying what you want to create, why, and how to bring it into existence, and in doing so, you will be exercising your right to determine your future. Such clarity empowers and emboldens us to take a stand, express our point of view, take-action, and argue for what is right and just.

The *Seven-Step Guide to Plan for Self-Determination* is organized in three main sections:

1. Developing Your Plan
2. Implementing Your Plan
3. Building Human and Organizational Capacity

It will provide you with seven major steps and guidelines to develop your plans, successfully execute them, improve the effectiveness of your organizational system and processes, and develop a high-performance organization. In summary, to create and determine the future you desire.

All people have a right to determine their future.
Marcelene Anderson

Dedication

I dedicate this book to the Dakhota* people whose original homeland was Southern Minnesota, where I grew up. Through my heart and mind connection with the Dakhota, I join with the Indigenous people everywhere in recognizing that we are all related, or as the Oglala Sioux say, *mitaku oyasin:*

"Let us work together for cultural reclamation, self-determination, and sovereignty, to heal and honor Mother Earth".

*Dakhota is the original spelling that the people used, and today we tend to see it spelled without the 'h'. Source— Minnesota Historical Society. Additionally, I have discovered that Dakota means "allies, friends."

Contents

Preface

The future is in our hands,
and we are not hapless bystanders.

We can influence whether we have a
planet of peace, social justice, equity,
and growth or earth of unbridgeable
differences between peoples, wasted
resources, corruption, and terror."

James D. Wolfensohn
from "A Better World Is Possible,"
(July-Aug 2003) The Futurist Quote of the Year

As a practical futurist and a system thinker, Marcelene Anderson has written this book as a guide for leaders and people who want to create a better future, envisioning and realizing it. We live in a new era that requires new ideas, fresh solutions, and approaches from strategic thinking and a future-focused orientation.

This book is for leaders who are dissatisfied with the status quo and want to make a difference. It will provide them with a systematic process to determine the future, the results they want, and successfully implement their plans. Additionally, it will guide them to create highly effective organizations where employees are engaged, motivated, and work together to achieve results consistently.

Acknowledgment

I owe a great deal to the Dakota tribe. More than words can convey. As the original inhabitants of Turtle Island, their significant loss was other people's gain, including mine. My connection with the Dakota has opened my heart and awareness about Indigenous people everywhere and to an ongoing lifelong journey and commitment to collaborate with leaders who are ready and already writing the next chapter of history.

Growing up I learned very little about the history of Indigenous peoples, their cultures, political structures, contributions, etc. Over time, I chose to remedy this with ongoing learning to this day.

Similarly, I knew very little about planning in the early years of my career. Initially, I doubted my ability to lead planning sessions. Gradually, over many years, I learned and developed planning skills, beginning by planning, and leading a conversation with a single group to determine next steps. Eventually, I learned how to develop strategic plans, including a purpose and mission statement, creating a future vision, identifying obstacles to the vision, developing strategies and actions to overcome obstacles and close gaps and the need for action plans to realize desired results. Ultimately, I realized planning was not enough and that a plan needed an effective implementation system.

When I started to build my planning skills 40 years ago, there was no internet to google specific topics or find resources, and there were few books to help me. I learned through trial and error and continued to explore and experiment with various planning approaches and systems that enabled me to develop my hybrid strategic planning and implementation system.

I am also indebted to the late Stephen Haines, CEO of the Haines Centre for Strategic Management, for his work in translating, planning, and implementing research into an integrated, practical planning, implementation, change management, and leadership development process.

As part of my 18 year-long learning process I was fortunate to have met, studied, and worked with the late Stephen Haines, CEO of the Haines Centre for Strategic Management. He translated, planned, and implemented research into an integrated, practical planning, implementation, change management and leadership development process. When I read his book, The Systems Thinking Approach to Strategic Management, I realized it articulated what I had been attempting to do with my clients for years. Subsequently, I went on to acquire the Gold Level Systems Thinking and Strategic Management Certificate and worked as a partner with the Haines Centre for several rewarding years.

I also wish to pay tribute to the Institute for Cultural Affairs (ICA), with whom I worked as a volunteer and National Director for ten years. I participated in research to develop methodologies and processes to assist communities and organizations worldwide to take charge of their future and transform people's lives and communities.

The ICA methods laid the foundation for me to become a systems thinker, developing participation skills and consensus methods to engage people in planning for their future.

I owe special thanks to Susan Anderson, More Than Words Consulting, for her invaluable skills in editing my book.

In addition, I wish to acknowledge my clients with whom I have had the opportunity to share with them and deepen my understanding of best practices for being future-focused and results-oriented. I am grateful for the opportunity to assist them in realizing a better future and more significant results. Together, we have applied vital principles and best practices for planning, implementation, and building high-performance organizations. I have also expanded my knowledge and gained valuable wisdom from our collaborations.

I hope this book will guide you in planning for self-determination and realizing the future you want to bring into being and the results you want to achieve as an organization.

Introduction:
Why Strategic Planning is
Vital to Achieving Results

If you don't have a plan for your
future, someone else will.

Marcelene Anderson

In a recent survey of business leaders, including Fortune 500 companies and a wide range of organizations, participants identified strategic planning as one of the three most important activities for the future.

Self Determination requires long-term
thinking, a vision, goals, strategies,
and a solid plan to realize it.

Planning for the future is especially vital for Indigenous nations to determine their future and become increasingly self-sufficient, once again.

Effective organizations, like individuals, plan for tomorrow and act in the present.

Strategic Planning is simply a thinking process; it allows a board of directors or council, management, employees, and citizens to consider possible alternatives, focus on the future direction, and develop strategies and plans to achieve in future.

A strategic plan serves as a roadmap to the desired future. In addition, it allows planning for the strategic allocation of resources. A solid plan provides a framework for decision-making on an ongoing basis, setting guidelines for what decision-makers will do and not do, what they will invest in and not.

Strategy is about making choices, trade-offs; it's about deliberately choosing to be different.

Michael E. Porter

This book will provide you with a systematic process and best practices for creating robust strategic plans if you are: the Chief of an Indigenous nation or tribe or organization, the President of a midsized business, the founder of an entrepreneurial enterprise, or a division of a Fortune 500 company.

Purposes of Strategic Planning:
- To proactively plan the future of the organization
- To think together about the future of the organization and get everyone 'on the same page
- To make decisions and set priorities on how to use resources strategically
- To translate hopes and dreams for the organization into concrete and achievable action or work plans to realize the strategic direction

"The future is not some place we are going, but one we are creating. The paths are not to be found but made. The activity of making them changes both the maker and their destination."

~ John Schaar

More than Planning is Needed to Achieve Results

As important as planning is, it is not enough. It is essential to consistently implement your plan to move closer to your desired future and goals.

Additionally, it is vital to build a high-performance organization with the systems and employee capabilities that will enable the organization to achieve 100% of its goals. In the Systems Thinking Approach to Strategic Planning, Stephen Haines says that:

- Developing a strategic, operational, and annual plan is vital but it only moves an organization 20% of the way to its desired future
- Successfully implementing a plan enables an organization to move another 40% towards its desired future
- Building a high-performance organization with systems to attract and retain, engage, develop talent, provide regular feedback, compensate fairly enables the organization to achieve the final 40%

In other words, an organization needs a total Strategic Management System that integrates planning + implementation + change + leadership.

My Creating Results System, based on Strategic Management principles, is a comprehensive system that leads, manages, and changes your organization in a conscious, well-planned, integrated fashion. It is based on your core strategies to achieve your desired future vision and results or goals. It is a complete integrated planning system, including a multi-year strategic plan with annual plans, departmental and individual employee plans, and strategic budgets and measurements.

According to the research of McKinsey and Company, which surveyed executives of some 150 companies of multi-business companies report on how the executives approach the development of corporate strategy. More than a quarter of the executives surveyed say their organizations lack a consistent process for developing strategy. Executives at companies that are robust strategy developers are twice as likely as their peers to say their companies apply a distinct corporate strategy process.

A synthesis of more than two decades on the merits of strategic planning carried out by Chet Miller and Laura Cardinal determined that strategic planning positively affects the performance of organizations. They initially argued that planning had a more significant impact on performance in large rather than in small firms, and to a greater extent, in capital-intensive rather than labor-intensive firms. However, their current findings suggest that planning affects performance equally in large and small, and capital intensive and labor-intensive firms.

Over the past thirty years, I have researched, learned, and applied several recognized planning processes, in addition to those I developed my own. These include the ICA Workshop Method, Future Search, Preferred Futuring, the Search Conference, and the Systems Thinking Approach® to

Strategic Management. Based on my research and experience, the most comprehensive and effective planning systems integrate planning and implementation. By comparison, earlier generation planning processes focused primarily on creating a budget for the coming year.

Planning for a Complex Environment

Organizations of all types face complex issues and challenges, making planning far more difficult. Khris Dunn from the HR Capitalist expressed it succinctly—complexity is the enemy of getting things done. Today's complexities demand a system-wide perspective versus an analytical approach, addressing each problem and situation separately.

My clients have endorsed the benefits of adopting and applying systems thinking in their organizations. They have found that their planning efforts produce better results. Employees are better situated to implement changes in their strategic and organizational plans from one year to the next versus each department creating plans in isolation and using different planning models.

Humankind has not woven the web of life.
We are but one thread within it.
Whatever we do to the web, we do to ourselves.
All things are bound together. All things connect.

Chief Seattle

The Creating Results System™

Insanity, according to Albert Einstein, is doing the same thing repeatedly and expecting different results. Many leaders are caught in the same results trap, continually doing the same things, hoping the results will change. The solution to this dilemma is to think different thoughts and take other actions.

One of the most significant breakthroughs in thinking and guiding change in organizations comes from systems theory and systems thinking, Professor Jay Forrester at MIT in 1956. Like a car, which is an organized collection of parts that have been integrated into a functioning whole, a system is a collection of related elements (various inputs which go through specific processes to produce certain outputs) organized into a complex whole.

From an organizational standpoint, a system comprises many smaller systems or subsystems, such as administrative and management functions, products, services, groups, and individuals. If one part of the system is changed, the nature of the overall design is often changed as well.

A high-functioning system also includes a feedback loop for monitoring and evaluating the system's inputs, throughputs to outcomes. This continuous exchange of feedback among its various parts ensures that they remain closely aligned and focused on achieving the desired goal of the system.

We are what we think. All that we
are arises with our thoughts. With our
thoughts, we make the world.

The Buddha

The Creating Results Seven-Step Process

When applied to strategic planning, the systems thinking approach answers seven strategic thinking questions:

Step 1. Environmental Scan—What future trends will likely impact our organization in the next five to ten years? If these trends did occur, what would the impact be?

Outputs
Step 2. Desired Future—What is our mission, vision, and our values? How relevant are they for our future world/ environment?

Measurement
Step 3. Feedback—How will we know when we've gotten there? How will we measure progress towards our desired future?

Inputs
Step 4. Current Situation—Where are we today? What are the gaps between where we want to be in the future and where we are now?

Step 5. Strategies—How will we close the gaps between where we want to be and where we are now? What strategies and strategic actions do we need to take in the next three years to achieve our desired future?

Throughputs
Step 6. Implementation—What actions or projects do we need to take in the next three years to achieve our mission, vision, and performance targets/goals? As well, what strategies and strategic actions do we need to take in the next three years to make progress towards our desired future?

Step 7- Annual Strategic Plan Review and Update- Why is it crucial to review and update your strategic plan annually? What are its two goals? Who should be involved? How to review and update the plan?

See Figure 1, below.

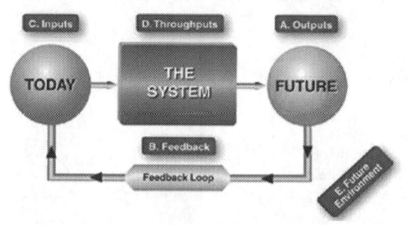

Figure 1: Creating Results Program based on Systems Thinking
Used with permission, Haines Centre for Strategic Management

According to Peter Senge, author of The Fifth Discipline, Systems thinking said,

> *"A shift of mind from seeing parts to seeing wholes,*
> *from seeing people as helpless reactors to seeing*
> *them as active participants in shaping their reality,*
> *from reacting to the present to creating the future."*

Benefits of the Creating Results System™

The Creating Results Strategic Management Process produces a multi-year plan that includes:

- The future trends likely to impact the organization.
- A purpose, mission, and vision for the next three or more years.
- Core values that reflect the behaviors/norms of the organization.

- Key success measures, performance indicators, its targets to track progress toward the vision and mission.
- An assessment of the gaps between where the organization wants to be and where it currently is.
- A set of core strategies (or objectives) that can be implemented across the business units/departments, providing consistency and flexibility.
- Priorities for action in the coming year and the next three years or more.
- Action or work plans to realize the year-one priorities, including strategic budgets.
- A high-level implementation timeline and calendar.
- A systematic process to successfully implement the multi-year plan, monitor progress, and make continuous improvements.
- A process to update the strategic plan annually or more frequently.
- A plan to develop and sustain a high-performance organization that can achieve results over time.

What You Can Expect to Get Out of this Book

Strategic thinking and ideas generated are critical factors for creating a desired new future and results. This book explains how to generate ideas and transform them into proactive, strategic, achievable, practical plans. It also describes how several organizations achieved breakthrough, sustainable results by new thinking and doing things differently. The book is our shared story.

As a management consultant for 40 years, I could not have done this without working collaboratively with leaders who wanted to break out of the same results syndrome, achieve a better future and more significant results. Similarly, I believe these clients would not have attained these new results without new thinking and willingness to do things differently.

Within these pages, you will hear the stories of remarkable organizations such as:

- An Indigenous tribe had been forced to leave their community—how families were divided and forced to live apart for over four years. You will learn how they came together to envision a new future, which resulted in a model community.
- A division of a Fortune 500 company created when the corporation acquired other companies and brands. Despite excellent products, this division was not meeting its corporate targets. You will learn how they went from not achieving their targets to achieving them for the first time and ultimately, winning the President's award for "Best Performing Division" in its category in North America.
- An Indigenous economic development organization with an incredible vision to foster self-sufficiency in its community over the next 25 years. You will learn how they became a future-focused and results-based organization that achieved 100% of its objectives in year one and consistently achieved its targets year after year.
- A department of a global telecom organization whose leader realized that his department needed to restructure, refocus, and realign itself to changing business strategies and meet the changing needs of clients. You will learn how employee skepticism is transformed through engagement in the process

and how, within six months, they were ahead in the implementation of their plan.

- An Indigenous holding company, after operating its original four core businesses for several decades, diversified and expanded its businesses.
- An innovative not-for-profit educational science program with rapid growth needed a plan for growth and expansion. The first plan was built on the organization's achievements and strengths, providing a shared vision and an initial road map for development. The subsequent plan included a vision for national growth and metrics for measuring progress.

I have had the opportunity of working with hundreds of diverse organizations across private and not-for-profit sectors and industries. In addition, I have had the privilege of working collaboratively with Indigenous organizations that wanted to create a better future for their citizens.

A common thread among these organizations was that they wanted to achieve more significant results and committed to doing the necessary work. They were looking for the "holy grail" to a better future with sustainable results and created a roadmap for getting there.

The strategic management process is for leaders of Indigenous organizations and others:

1. Those not satisfied with the status quo and believe your organization can do much better.
2. Tired of being unfocused and reactive.
3. Dealing with an organization unaligned towards a shared future direction and achieving inconsistent results.

This process will provide you with a future-focused and results-based approach to planning and execution, all the while engaging the human spirit and creative energy of employees at all levels. By applying The Creating Results Strategic Management Process, you will identify and create the desired future for yourself and your organization.

Chapter 1:
Why A Future-Focused Approach To Planning?

Although every organization wants to achieve great things, many work day-to-day without future planning. Additionally, they do not know how to implement their plans to achieve results. Some are stuck in the "Same Results Syndrome" caused by many factors. The following is a list of the most common ones found in organizations:

1. Being unaware of the larger future environment in which the organization operates (this is like having your head in the sand).
2. An unclear vision of where the organization wants to be in the future.
3. Not measuring progress consistently in critical areas of importance to the organization and only measuring financial performance.
4. Being unaware, unclear, and or in denial about the gaps and obstacles between where the organization wants to be and where it is today.
5. Being unfocused and reactive, trying to do too many things.
6. Not having a set of core strategies to close the gaps and circumvent the obstacles blocking the desired future (mission, vision, and values).

7. Being misaligned across the organization, e.g., each department has different objectives, which may conflict.
8. Not being aligned down the organization, e.g., employees do not understand the link between the mission and vision of the organization and what they do day-to-day.
9. Attempting to implement too many actions or projects at once without prioritizing them as well as organizing them in a multi-year sequence.
10. The absence of detailed action plans which lack specificity, e.g., What, How, When and How Much.
11. Leaving implementation of action priorities to chance.
12. Developing a strategic plan and not following through.
13. Not monitoring progress frequently to consistently learning what is working and not.
14. Leadership is uncommitted to the strategic plan, e.g., not walking the talk.
15. Not providing resources for others to take needed action.
16. Allowing the strategic plan to become stale and irrelevant by waiting too long to update it.
17. Disengaged employees.
18. Missing or ineffective systems which support high performance.

The Creating Results Scorecard™

To help you identify areas where your organization is doing well and areas for improvement, complete The Creating Results Scorecard, Figure 2, on the next page. Rate your organization on each of the ten continuums, between 1 to 5. Add up your total for each column.

We do not have a clear direction and vision for the future of our organization	1	2	3	4	5	We have a clear direction and vision for our future
We are unfocused and reactive	1	2	3	4	5	We are focused & proactive
We are unaligned at various levels of the business	1	2	3	4	5	We are aligned at all levels of the business
We are wasting time and resources	1	2	3	4	5	We are effectively using our time and resources
Employees are disengaged and or lack motivation	1	2	3	4	5	Employees are highly engaged/motivated
We don't have an up-to-date strategic and operational plan	1	2	3	4	5	We have an up-to-date strategic and operational plan
We do not have a systematic process to monitor results	1	2	3	4	5	We have an effective systematic process to monitor results
Our organizational culture (the way we do things) does not support our goals	1	2	3	4	5	Our organizational culture (the way we do things) supports our goals
Departments and employees do not have goals aligned with the vision and mission of the organization	1	2	3	4	5	Departments and employees have goals aligned with the vision and mission of the organization
We do not consistently reach our goals	1	2	3	4	5	We consistently achieve our goals
ADD COLUMN TOTALS						YOUR SCORE _____ 50

Figure 2: The Creating Results Scorecard™

The Creating Results Scorecard Rating

1–9 Significant improvement required

10-24 Ongoing improvement required

25-39 Making progress – Target key areas for improvement

40-50 Well on your way to become a high-performing organization

Whatever your rating, the remainder of the book will help you take your organization to the next level. The subsequent chapters will provide you and your organization with a practical and robust step-by-step process to focus the direction you want to go, align your organization, and engage employees to make sustainable leaps in results and growth.

As a result of applying this process, your organization will achieve sustainable growth and move toward reaching its full potential. Your leaders, management, and staff will be more engaged, and your reputation as a quality employer will grow.

With your organization aligned at all levels, and organizational culture to match your goals, you will save time and money and hopefully be excited, inspired, and confident that you are moving forward. And, most importantly, you will be more focused, proactive, and able to seize new opportunities to grow. Moreover, you will have a plan for self-determination.

The future doesn't just happen—decisions shape it.

- Paul Tagliabue (1940 -) NFL Commissioner

Section 1:

Developing
Your Plan

Chapter 2: Preparing-to-Plan

Getting ready to plan

Success is 95% preparation. – Author unknown

Starting a project, such as strategic planning, is often challenging. The temptation is to begin, hoping everything will fall into place, but they seldom do.

Unfortunately, many organizations jump into planning without taking time to get ready. It is like the adage that management guru Tom Peters talked about years ago. He found many companies practiced "fire, aim and ready" to capitalize on opportunities. They had jumped into and acted, versus a "ready, aim and fire" approach. Re-active-oriented organizations tend to use the fire and then aim approach before getting ready.

A better way is to remember, **Success is planned...in advance!**

Research also says that every hour spent in preparation saves time carrying out tasks.

The goal of the Prepare-to-Plan step is to get educated, organized, and tailor the planning process for the organization.

Checklist for Preparing to Plan

You might be wondering what is important to include for a successful strategic planning and implementation process.

From years of planning experience and research, the checklist below outlines essential tasks and considerations to plan for successful outcomes:

- ❑ Determine what levels of the organization for which you are planning
- ❑ Establish a core planning team who have responsibility for input into the planning and implementation process
- ❑ Educate the core planning team, so they have a shared understanding of the planning and implementation process
- ❑ Identify the key issues you want the planning to address
- ❑ Determine the outcomes you want to achieve
- ❑ Choose a theme for the planning and implementation process to provide focus
- ❑ Determine the best planning approach for the outcomes you want to achieve
- ❑ Create a schedule for the entire planning process at all levels
- ❑ Identify who you want to engage in the planning and implementation process
- ❑ Secure senior management commitment to the strategic management process
- ❑ Designate funding upfront to support the implementation of the plans
- ❑ Develop promotional plans for engaging stakeholders
- ❑ Reserve adequate space and arrange for equipment necessary for the event and participant care strategies
- ❑ Determine essential roles: organizational leadership for the event; primary facilitator; breakout group facilitators; greeters at the door to welcome people; technical coordinator; refreshment coordinator;

administration coordinator; on-site Health and Safety Coordinator: overall coordination for the event. Note: The number of participants at the event will determine how many of these critical roles will be needed

❑ Brief all persons about their roles and responsibilities

This chapter goes into more detail about the importance of each of the above and how to do them.

Task 1: Determine Levels Of Planning

Leaders must first decide the level for which they are planning, e.g., for the organization, its departments, the employees, or all of them.

Organizations such as First Nations or tribal governments may wish to start the process by engaging their community members in the process. See Figure3.

Figure 3: Five Level Integrated Planning

Regardless of the level, you are planning or all levels, it is essential to have alignment across all levels or functions. To align all levels, cascade your organization's plan to your departments and or business units, where strategy is turned into action to bring about results and anticipated changes realized.

> *Cooperation gets teams pulling together. Staying*
> *focused on the organization's mission ensures*
> *they pull together in the right direction.*

Eric Harvey

The next and subsequent chapters describe Planning for the Community (Level 1) and other levels in more detail.

Task 2: Preliminary Tasks

Before jumping into the Prepare-To-Plan step, there are essential tasks to be carried out. Working through these tasks will position you for tremendous success in the overall planning process.

2.1 Conduct a Strategic Assessment of the Organization

Getting a realistic overview of how your organization has been working and what needs to be changed is an essential first step. To achieve this, conduct an overall assessment of your organization's present situation before your Plan-to-Plan day. Determine the kinds of strategies you are currently using and whether they are worth keeping or should be updated.

2.2 Select & Educate the Core Planning Team – Plan to Plan Day

For planning to be successful, select persons who represent the levels for which you are planning, providing relevant input. Preparing to plan entails educating the planning team on the planning process and developing their commitment to the process.

We recommend holding an off-site Plan-to-Plan session with the Core Planning Team. Half of the session focuses on educating them about strategic management, and the other half on organizing and tailoring the planning process for your organization and the level(s) for which you are planning.

2.3 Identify Key Issues to be Addressed in the Planning Process

One of the critical topics of the Core Planning Team in the one-day Plan-to-Plan session is identifying key issues the plan needs to address.

Gather concerns or problems from various stakeholders in the community. Undoubtedly, they will have a diverse range of opinions and concerns to share.

Prioritizing the list of issues is an important step to focus on planning.

2.4 Tailor the Planning Process for Your Organization

The Core Planning Teams needs to address the critical aspects of the planning process, such as:

- ❏ Developing key performance indicators and goals to monitor progress
- ❏ Creating strategies to close the gaps between where it wants to be in the future and currently is
- ❏ Putting in place a consistent implementation process

To assist organizations with prioritizing areas of concern, "The Creating Results Scorecard" helps assess your current planning process and identify specific areas to strengthen. If you have not already completed the Scorecard, you may want to go back to page 3 above before reading further.

Review your current mission, vision, and values with the Core Planning Team to ensure a shared understanding. These may need to be updated. You may also need to focus on areas missing from your plan, e.g., a scan of future environmental trends and key performance indicators.

Tailoring your strategic management process for your organization provides the core planning team with a way to focus on what's important.

2.5 Introduce Environmental Scanning

Another critical area to introduce with the Core Planning Team is Environmental Scanning, identifying trends likely to impact the organization for the time horizon for your plan, e.g., 3, 5, 10 years. For example, if you envision the next five years, you would research trend forecasts for the next five years.

Environmental Scanning is essential so that you do not create your strategic plan in a vacuum with the illusion that future conditions will be the same as today. If you are planning only for the present, you plan for the past, as today will be the past as soon as tomorrow. Therefore, it is essential to anticipate future trends likely to impact your community or organization.

Stephen Haines introduced me to a helpful framework, SKEPTIC, for researching and tracking environmental trends.

The "S" stands for socio-demographic trends "K" stands for your competitors. "E" stands for economic as well as the environment. "P" stands for political. "T" for technology. "I" your industry. And "C" for your customers/ clients.

Although the SKEPTIC framework provides a comprehensive framework for planning, you may wish to tailor your research framework for your community and organization.

In Preparing to Plan, the Core Planning Team and volunteers in your organization research the trends most likely to impact your community or organization, to come to the planning session ready to share their findings.

Without considering the future environment, the danger is you are planning in a vacuum without facts and figures on environmental changes you can expect. You will end up preparing for the present, not the future. As a result, your plan will not have a roadmap to your desired future.

Chapter 4, Environmental Scanning, will cover this process in more detail.

Task 3: Tailor The Planning Process For Your Organization

3.1 Develop a theme for the planning and implementation process

Before developing the schedule, create a theme for the planning event that focuses the spirit and intent of the planning and implementation.

3.2 Scheduling the Planning the Process

A vital component of the getting ready to plan step is creating a schedule for the sessions and organizing the details. Developing a clear timetable for the planning process is essential to avoid getting bogged down. Employees are often preoccupied with work or have made other commitments, causing delays and gaps in the planning process.

Scheduling in advance is vital. Create, post, and share an organizational calendar, asking all managers and employees to block out these special days in their agendas. Send periodic reminders to treat these dates as sacred.

3.3 Secure Commitment to the Planning Process

Leadership must communicate the importance of attendance, participation, and honoring the time commitment required by doing so themselves. Failure to demonstrate their commitment to the planning process and set expectations for all managers and employees to actively participate puts the results at risk.

Agreement on how the plan will cascade down and across the organization is crucial at this stage, from the community to the organization, then to departments to develop its departmental strategic plan, aligned with the organizational plan; then employee planning, and creating a strategic budget budget and a strategic management calendar for the year.

In a final session, review the plans of all the departments to ensure plans are aligned with the overall organizational strategy and address community priorities.

Recognize this is a long-term effort to put your strategic management system in place. In some cases, it may require as much as two annual planning and budgeting cycles to complete.

The planning team and organizational leadership are responsible for developing a timeline with the when and how.

Task 4: Establish An Internal Support Team

It would help if you chose individuals for your internal support team who will be committed to working collaboratively throughout the planning and implementation process. They are accountable for the success of the planning process and should be chosen early in the process. According to Stephen Haines, there is an element of capacity building to be "engineered" upfront to ensure ongoing support, persistence, and coordination of senior management and core planning team.

It may be that the organization lacks the leadership skills to develop and execute the plan. Conducting a leadership assessment helps identify skills gaps and ensure the management team is willing to develop needed skills to guide the organization through planning and implementation steps. Therefore, a workshop or leadership training session may be a prerequisite to the strategic planning and implementation process.

4.1 Leadership Commitment

Your organization's Chief or the CEO are the individuals who need to set the example for others. They have the responsibility and authority (in conjunction with the Council's or Board of Director's consent and veto power) to make decisions and move the process forward. It is not enough to delegate this responsibility to departmental heads or committees. They need to demonstrate commitment to the planning process and the subsequent implementation of the plan by remaining active and involved from start to finish. Otherwise, the process will fail.

I've worked with organizations where a high level of management commitment to planning and implementation has been in place. In these cases, the planning process has been highly effective. I have also worked with organizations where senior leaders authorized the planning but did not participate in sessions. Because they didn't have "ownership" for the plan, they were not committed, and subsequently, good plans were not implemented.

Task 5: Plan To Engage Key Stakeholders

To achieve buy-in to your strategic plan, involving individuals who will make decisions about it and implement it is crucial. With early engagement, they are more likely to support it. If you haven't engaged their hearts and minds, they're unlikely to endorse the plan, and, therefore, the plan has a low chance of success.

People tend to work harder for their ideas.
Solutions they participate in developing
become commitments that are much more
likely to yield quick and permanent results.

Eric Harvey

After you have identified key stakeholders whose input, feedback, and support are important, consider the best options for involving them in the planning process.

---

*Tip: People are more likely to support
that which they help to create*

For example, a Council or a Board of Directors can be involved in the initial process of developing strategy but do not need to be involved in departmental planning and implementation.

Level 1: Chapter 4 will explore options for engaging community members or stakeholders in the planning process.

5.1 Engage Stakeholders in Using the Parallel Process

Another way of engaging stakeholders in planning is using what Stephen Haines calls a 'Parallel Process'. This involves engaging stakeholders in giving input about the plan as it is being developed. Conduct the 'parallel' process simultaneously as the plan is developed, in contrast with approaches where stakeholders wait until the plan is completed before asking for their feedback.

To accomplish this, identify stakeholders to engage in the Parallel Process during the planning phase. It is helpful to decide how and where to engage stakeholders in parallel planning. For example, during the organizational planning phase, as you develop or update documents related to the Desired Future, e.g., purpose, mission, vision, and values, you may wish to get feedback from your stakeholders using a Parallel Process. If necessary, break a large group of participants into smaller groups to make it easier to facilitate and capture their feedback.

Invite stakeholders to give feedback with the promise that all input will be heard and seriously considered. Caution them not to expect that their exact words will show up in the plan as feedback from all persons will be integrated.

Provide participants with an explanation of the strategic planning model and explain their role and contribution to the process. An education component to the Parallel Process is essential to ensure participants genuinely understand concepts, keywords, and intentions. Otherwise, you may find yourselves working at odds with one another.

You may use this approach anywhere throughout the planning process. In addition to the Desired Future, it can be helpful when developing your Feedback System, or your Key Success Measures and targets, as well as the strategies you develop.

The feedback from the Parallel Process will confirm if your stakeholders (community members, staff, or other interested parties) think/feel you are going in the right direction or if modification is needed. In addition, you will likely get valuable insights and suggestions. Remember that people tend to accept change more readily when they decide what needs to happen.

The Parallel Process feedback is reviewed and considered by the Planning Team, who decide whether or not to integrate the input into the plan. Share the final strategic plan is with all those who participated in the Parallel Process.

Task 6: Create A Shared Understanding Of The Process

Many managers will have worked in other organizations and learned different planning terminology, e.g., mission, vision, and strategies, etc. Establishing shared vocabulary is essential to ensure everyone has the same frame of reference to participate fully in the process.

An organization has two options for educating managers. One way is to hold a pre-planning education session to familiarize managers with the planning process. In addition, another approach is to incorporate brief education moments throughout the entire planning process. Both may be done as managers are learning the planning process.

Task 7: Other Considerations

7.1 Plan to Integrate Your Budget with Your Strategic Planning

Some organizations let their budgets dictate their planning boundaries or constraints. In addition, consider your organization's financial resources and assess its future priorities. The challenge is finding a balance between both.

An additional option is to review your present budget allocations, then determine which items can be eliminated to free up resources for higher priorities. Chapter 15 discusses creating a strategic budget to implement your strategic plan's priorities.

7.2 Commit Resources

Securing in advance the resources needed for the implementation of the plan is essential. Not having resources committed wastes everyone's time and effort, only to have the plan sit on a shelf, which demotivates everyone involved and leads to profound disappointment.

Ensuring commitment of resources starts with your organization's Leadership Team. They are the ones who have the authority and power to make decisions about the allocation of dollars to projects and initiatives that support their strategic priorities. Therefore, it is essential to begin addressing the budget issue with the core planning team at the start of the process. If the leadership team is unwilling to commit resources to support the strategic plan, it puts the plan's success at risk.

One of the critical errors organizations frequently make is not allowing sufficient time to plan and integrate it with budgeting. A lot of time goes into developing and completing your strategic plan, and you do not want to rush completing the budgeting process, as plans require resources to carry them out. When designing your Planning Schedule, include sufficient time to create your strategic plan and a strategic budget to support it.

7.3 Select an External Facilitator

In addition to the internal coordinator, most organizations need an unbiased external professional facilitator to guide you through the strategic management process, facilitating it for at least the first 3 years planning cycle as you and your organization learn and implement the strategic management process. It is not easy to navigate differing opinions and perspectives fairly and impartially. Yet a good facilitator can keep the process moving forward and helping the team to make difficult choices.

According to Haines, in addition to having the ability to play devil's advocate, the facilitator should have several other qualifications, including, among other things:

- Strong business, economic, and industry experience
- An understanding of group dynamics and human behavior
- Good knowledge of large-scale change and transition management
- A breadth of strategic planning and project management experience.

7.4 Develop Internal Facilitation Capability

In addition to finding the right external facilitator to guide and lead your planning process, developing internal facilitation capacity is vital to ensure you have the resources needed to lead the various planning tasks and processes over time.

Recap: Checklist For Getting Ready To Plan

❑ Leadership commitment is secured.
❑ The Core Planning Team has been selected, educated, and engaged in planning and organizing the planning process.
❑ Key issues are determined.
❑ Vital outcomes for planning are pinpointed.
❑ The levels to be engaged in planning are established.
❑ Priorities for developing your plan is determined using the Scorecard.
❑ A theme is chosen for the planning process.
❑ Leadership assesses the organization's present planning capability.
❑ An assessment of the organization and its systems is carried out.
❑ The capacity of the management team assessed.

❑ The planning process is mapped out to achieve the desired outcomes; a schedule established, and time committed.

❑ Environmental Scanning research roles have been agreed to.

❑ People are invited who need to be involved.

❑ All who will be involved are actively engaged in the process.

❑ Resources for implementing the plans are committed.

❑ A professional facilitator is engaged.

❑ Internal resource persons are trained to assist with the planning process, lead and guide the organization.

Success is planned in advance

Chapter 3:
Step 1: Scanning for Future Trends
Adapting to a changing environment

Identifying likely future environmental trends is a vital part of Preparing to Plan. Many people believe that climate change is a recent development. The truth is that scientists began warning of climate change over fifty years ago. Their predictions of growing holes in the ozone and the disappearance of species seemed bizarre, was largely ignored for decades. Today we can no longer ignore climate change or say that it isn't happening, as we are experiencing the effects and impact of climate change everywhere, every day.

Figure 4: Scan the Future Environment for Trends

Consider what happens before and during an airline flight.

Air traffic control verifies the weather conditions, the direction, and velocity of the wind, temperatures, potential storm conditions, etc. They also check the conditions at the destination and along the flight path. Air traffic control then develops a flight plan to take passengers safely to their destination. If they did not consider these factors in creating a flight plan, you and I would consider it irresponsible and dangerous. We trust that this has happened behind the scenes.

Similarly, organizations need to consider the larger external environment— it can be detrimental not to.

For example, let's look at the automotive industry. A few years ago, the automotive industry was impacted by rising petroleum prices, creating a demand for fuel-efficient vehicles. Failure to look ahead puts an industry sector or organization at risk, as we have all witnessed repeatedly.

Environmental scanning of future trends helps an organization to move towards its desired future with confidence proactively. Once you have considered what's likely to happen in the larger environment, you can make strategic choices for the organization's well-being and growth. Organizations that foresee and adapt to the changing environment are the most likely to survive and thrive, and failure to do so puts them at risk.

What is a Trend?

A trend is a discernible pattern—the general direction of something moving. When you observe behaviors and events that happen repeatedly, they form a pattern or a trend.

Many trends, or patterns, can significantly impact your

organization. Monitoring trends on an ongoing basis and including them in your planning is crucial. Discerning emerging trends allows you to proactively manage your organization versus be reactive when the trend has fully emerged, potentially limiting your options. Organizations must have the capacity to adjust to a changing environment quickly.

Identifying trends and determining appropriate responses is vital for an organization and a society. In addition to climate change trends, we can see examples of trends in many different areas. For example, there has been an increased demand for larger homes occupied by fewer persons in North America. Additionally, there has been an increase in obese children, increased demand for fuel-efficient vehicles. A shift to a more casual mode of dress in the workplace, texting as a form of communication, and many more trends are prevalent in today's society.

Trends ranging from macroeconomic, social, and business are shaping the global landscape. By anticipating the trends likely to impact them, an organization can ride the current rather than swim against it. According to Wendy Becker and Vanessa Freeman, authors of Going from Global Trends to Corporate Strategy published in The McKinsey Quarterly, an executive's ability to read trends accurately in a rapidly changing business environment can make all the difference between success and failure. Leaders must understand trends and the sub-trends behind each and how they are likely to impact their industry.

Just as airlines scan for relevant information regarding weather conditions, wind direction, velocity, temperature, and the presence of other aircraft while en-route, an organization must scan its environment for new or changing trends that can impact its future.

I consulted and licensed daycare providers early in my career, and I held sessions with them to plan for children's physical, mental, and social needs. I asked them to consider the future environment children were likely to grow up. After we explored the likely future environment, we then discussed how to prepare children for that future.

Although it was not a highly sophisticated process, it allowed us to work backward from the future to prepare children for the world in which they are likely to live.

We use a comprehensive environmental scanning acronym SKEPTIC, easy to remember from the Systems Thinking Approach to Strategic Planning by Stephen Haines. Each aspect of the SKEPTIC framework is described below:

Socio-Demographics—What social demographic changes are occurring or likely to occur in the next three years or more that could impact the organization?

Kompetition*—Who are our competitors likely to be in the next three years or more and what services and products will they likely offer?

Economy—What changes in the economy or financial sector are likely to occur that could impact the organization in the next three years or more?

Political—What political governance changes are likely to occur that could impact the organization in the next three years or more?

Technology—What technical changes are likely to occur that could impact the organization in the next three years or more?

Industry—What changes in our industry or sector are likely to occur that could impact the organization in the next three years or more?

Clients—Who are the clients/citizens likely to be in the next three years or more e.g., age, preferences, and so on?

***Note**—I have taken literary license here because I needed a 'K', in old English 'competition' was originally spelled with a 'K'.*

SKEPTIC Environmental Scan Worksheet		
Trend Categories	Trends likely to occur	Implications of the Trends
Socio-Demographics		
Competition		
Economy / Environment		
Political/ Governance		
Technology		
Industry		
Clients/Citizens		

Figure 5: Environmental Scan Worksheet

The SKEPTIC framework helps you think comprehensively about trends, organize them into meaningful clusters, and identify the likely implications so you can consider how best to address them in your future-focused plan.

Before starting organizational strategic planning, determining the environmental scanning framework factors to be used is an important consideration. We suggest using all the SKEPTIC elements. However, each organization must determine the Environmental factors most important to them.

Once you have agreed upon the factors to consider, assign them to specific individuals to research. Ask them to come prepared to present their findings on the likely future trends, along with the possible implications of these trends to your organization over the next three to ten years.

From my experience, dividing the trends categories among senior management or the planning team based on their interests is beneficial. As well, involve other employees in the organization who may be interested in a particular trend factor or category.

By dividing the trend factors between managers and other employees will allow more in-depth research of each trend factor and get better information. Allowing for different perspectives from various people and sources will only serve to strengthen your plan.

One challenge in the first year of environmental scanning is identifying helpful information sources. These will vary by the environmental factor. Possible sources include research organizations' reports such as *Aberdeen Research Report*, *The McKinsey & Co. Newsletter*, *The Economist*, government sources, Board of Trade research papers, *The Futurist Magazine*, and so on. Each organization and every industry have its specific research sources. Individuals who research trends in each category may want to consult industry directories or publications for pertinent information.

Once the environmental trends have been researched, compile them with possible implications into a summary, using the SKEPTIC framework.

Not all trends are of equal importance. By asking, "Of all these trends, which trends are most likely to occur, and which would have a high impact *if* they did occur?" you can take the discussion to another level. By focusing on a critical few, you can more effectively channel your energy and resources into proactive actions that will move the organization closer to its desired future.

Environmental scanning is not a once-a-year activity; it needs to be ongoing. I recommend that my clients report on trends monthly in their management teams, instilling this as an ongoing process in the organization.

One of my clients did this for several years and then discontinued the practice. When we updated their strategic plan recently, we noticed that very few managers and or employees had any new trends to report.

Without a system to scan for and report trends, putting your head in the sand is easy, resulting in being unprepared when they occur.

There are 3 kinds of people
- Those who make things happen
- Those who watch
- Those who wonder what happened

Anticipating future trends, what is going to happen, allows you to take action before it does, to prepare, adapt, and innovate.

People in your organization must constantly be scanning the larger environment, identifying trends that could impact the organization and their implications. By monitoring trends, the organization is always strategically prepared and proactive in dealing with its emerging future.

Recognizing that organizations have limited time and resources, focusing on the big questions, the most likely trends and how significant their impact can be will save time and money. Environmental scanning provides critical information for an organization to consider for its SWOT analysis.

It identifies future opportunities and threats that could either inhibit or threaten the organization's vision of future results.

Organizations are bombarded with many trends on an ongoing basis, see Figure 8, below. Although trends impact us, we do not have to be victims of them. Discerning the most important trends that are likely to affect them, particularly those which would have a high impact, allows an organization to seize opportunities and lessen threats. This will be discussed this further in the SWOT Analysis in the Chapter 6: Assessing Your Current Situation.

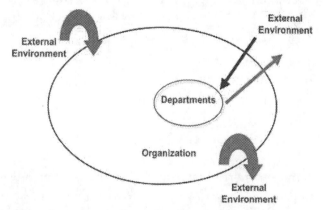

Figure 8: Example: Interaction with the Environment

As an organization is creating its strategic plan, it needs to consider the impact the environment will have on it and how it will impact the environment. Similarly, each business unit or department needs to consider trends likely to impact it and probable effects if they did occur. Consider the symbiotic relationship between an organization and the environment in which it operates. By doing so, the organization can take proactive actions to mitigate negative consequences associated with these critical trends.

According to the Institute for Public Policy research, identifying future opportunities rather than solving the past problems requires vigilance concerning trendspotting.

It can be tempting to succumb to a 'confirmation bias': a tendency to look for only those trends, information or data that support a point of view.

Trend experts note that change is often the result of a 'confluence of forces.' In determining trends, it is essential to determine whether there are enough different forces at play 'pushing in the same direction.'

Moreover, identifying trends may seem that pieces of information don't fit, are contradictory, or not related. But it is the connections between them that lead to the most revealing conclusions or questions. According to Mega Trends expert, John Naisbitt, the better we understand the relationships, the more accurate our picture will be. He suggests resisting the temptation of force-fitting meaning or connections between factors when a loose relationship might be the only conclusion to draw. Understanding the dynamics and interrelationships among trends can lead to more productive and relevant conclusions.

Although significant, unexpected, and unpredictable events can often disrupt our current reality, taking us in a new direction, the world moves more slowly than we sometimes acknowledge. While we cannot predict the future, trend analysis helps raise questions and provoke a discussion of possible directions and outcomes.

What to Consider:

- Environmental factors which are most relevant to the organization
- Assigning responsibility for researching and gathering data about likely future trends (three, five, ten years)
- Determining information sources to explore future trends
- Collecting likely future trends and determining the potential impact, both opportunities and threats

The greatest danger in times of turbulence is not the turbulence; it is to act with yesterday's logic.

Peter Drucker

LEVEL 1 - COMMUNITY PLANNING

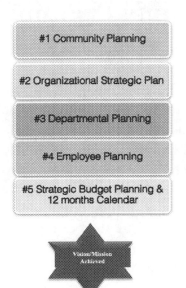

#1 Community Planning — Engage members in setting direction

#2 Organizational Strategic Plan — Create organizational strategic plan

#3 Departmental Planning — Align departments with organizational plan and create multi year plans

#4 Employee Planning — Set objectives to implement department priorities and key job description responsibilities and work plans

#5 Strategic Budget Planning & 12 months Calendar — Develop strategic budget to implement priorities and an annual calendar

Vision/Mission Achieved

The next chapter will provide a process about developing and engaging community members and stakeholders in planning for the community.

Chapter 4: Community Planning

Engage community members in setting direction

First Nations and tribal organizations are unique in recognizing their members as primary decision-makers for their communities or nations. This chapter explores options for engaging members and stakeholders in setting direction for the future of your nation and input for a community organization.

Community Planning

Developing a strategic plan for your nation or community is an opportunity to engage members of all ages, reinforcing their vital role in considering the community's future.

Too often, members think of themselves as bystanders as elected officials and administration staff make decisions. The goal of Community planning is to engage members in setting future direction for the community.

There are several ways, depending on what you want to achieve, the time and financial resources you have available.

Community Planning Options

- Celebrate the Community's Past
- Share Hopes and Dreams

- Identify Issues to Be Addressed
- Engage People of All Ages

Celebrate the Community's Past

*Before you know where you are going, you
must know where you have come.*

Author unknown

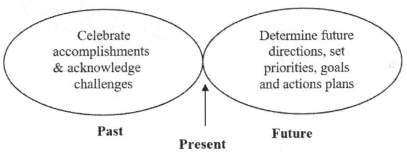

Past   Future
Present

Figure 7: Planning Timeframes

As an organization develops and or updates its strategic plan, it has an opportunity to assess and document its progress, achievements, key challenges, and significant events in its life to date. See Planning Timeframes, Figure 7, above.

Historical Scanning is a robust process that allows a group to tell and document its past collective shared story. It acknowledges their accomplishments and challenges, identifies important events and turning points in the life of the organization/community or nation. Moreover, it can position an organization in the broader historical context of the region or nation for a particular period.

Depicting and Documenting the Shared Story

Graphic Historical Story Telling

During the Historical Scan, participants create a "wall of wonder" depicting their shared story, e.g., the significant events, points where the community or organization has struggled, has been successful, etc. It provides an opportunity for remembering and reflection, for drawing out insights and learning for the future. It enables a group to see past the struggles they have faced, permitting them to reinterpret their history and to tell a new story about their resilience and adversity.

They might depict their story in a drawing and with words. The Cree Nation of Chisasibi created the forty-year Historical Scan shown in Figure 8 below.

Figure 8: Example: Cree Nation of Chisasibi Historical Scan

Alternatively, they can document their story in a chart which the Wawatay Communication Society did. See Figure 9 below.

Time frame	1970's	1980	1990-95	1996-2001
The Period	Giving Life	Growth Period	The Dark Ages	Reawakening
The Need / Opportunity	Vision to Preserve Our Language & Culture	Launched Radio & TV	Attempting New Ventures	Aware of Need to Change & Reorganize
Wawatay's Technological Role	Introduction of Technology to the NAN communities	Opening the Technological Window Wider	New Technological Changes Affecting Wawatay	Holding on, Needing to Innovate
Wawaty's Evolution	Wawatay Taking off	Wawatay Heyday	Wawatay Fell Behind	Trying to Catch Up
Wawaty's Market Role	Wawatay in Charge	Leadership Role	Loss of Control	Critical Stage

Figure 9: Example: Wawatay Communication Society Historical Scan
Used with permission of Wawatay
Communication Society. All rights reserved

Whichever approach is selected to depict the past, each process engages the group members in identifying critical periods, giving each period a name or title, telling a story about each period, and giving an overall title to the chapter in the life of the nation or organization. Inviting several persons to tell their story provides various perspectives of the organization's history or nation. Putting the story in writing ensures that the story is not lost.

My experience has shown that a Historical Scan fills gaps in what people know about the history of the community or organization, helping them to make sense of their past and understand how it got to be where it is today. Just like a human body holds pain internally, creating dis-ease, communities have pain from their past, blocking them from moving forward. The Historical Scan process allows a group to get in touch with their pain and externalize it through telling their stories. An additional optional step is holding a fire ceremony to release the pain to the fire, or they might choose other symbolic ways to release the past.

Honoring the past and all that has gone before is vital to release the human spirit to focus energy on the future.

Share Hopes and Dreams
Building on the Past and Future conversation, engage community members in sharing their hopes and dreams for the future of the community or nation and do the same for their family and themselves. Their hopes and dreams can be depicted in words or drawings, posted, and debriefed as a group to identify common themes and priorities.

Dreaming, after all, is a form of planning.

Gloris Steinem

Identify Issues to be Addressed
Members will identify current or future issues that could interfere with realizing their shared hopes and dreams. On a personal level, they will also do the same for their family and themselves.

This is an opportunity to explain the 5 Level Integrated Planning process, the 7-Step Creating Results process to members, and how they will be invited to provide critical feedback as the plan is being developed.

Engage People of All Ages
The above steps can be carried out individually or in facilitated focus groups such as elders, adults, business enterprises, stakeholders, etc.

Engage Elders in storytelling about your nation or community or share their wisdom with younger generations.

Engage youth in creating a play or drama about some aspect of your community or nation.

Tell children the nation's story. Engage them in depicting their visions of the community's future.

All the activities described in engaging people of all ages can be developed for families to do together to share in the future of the nation or community and their future as a family.

The Community planning events are a turning point for engaging members and stakeholders in a new future for their nation and themselves.

*Those who don't learn from the
past are likely to repeat it.*

Author Unknown

LEVEL 2 - ORGANIZATIONAL PLANNING

#1 Community Planning	Engage members in setting direction
#2 Organizational Strategic Plan	Create organizational strategic plan
#3 Departmental Planning	Align departments with organizational plan and create multi year plans
#4 Employee Planning	Set objectives to implement department priorities and key job description responsibilities and work plans
#5 Strategic Budget Planning & 12 months Calendar	Develop strategic budget to implement priorities and an annual calendar

Vision/Mission Achieved

The next chapter will explain the process, levels of planning and steps for developing the Organizational Strategic Plan.

Chapter 5: Step 2: Focusing Your Desired Future

Articulating your mission, core values, vision, and rallying cry

Just as your heart keeps you alive, three vital elements are at the heart of your strategic plan. These include a clear and powerful purpose, a compelling vision for the future, and strong core values. Without them, your plan will be nothing more than ideas on a piece of paper. Your mission, vision, and values provide meaning and spirit to your plan, essential to generating your desired results.

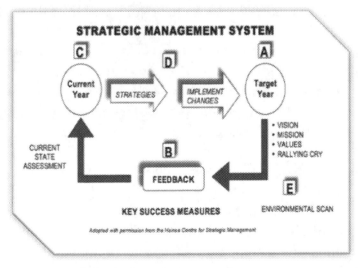

Figure 10: Begin with the End In Mind

This chapter has four sections:

A. Articulating Your Organization's Purpose and Mission
B. Focusing Compelling Shared Vision of the Desired Future
C. Stating Your Organization's Core Values
D. Creating Your Rallying Cry

A. Articulating Your Organization's Purpose and Mission

Purpose and Mission

Often the terms, "purpose" and "mission" are used interchangeably. In Built to Last, Collins and Porras, distinguish between the terms: they define purpose as true forever and mission as something important to achieve within a shorter duration. Although the terms mean something different, we will integrate purpose and mission for the sake of simplicity.

Just as an organization needs a clearly defined purpose, individuals need to know their life purpose. In his book, The Power of Purpose, Richard Leider says that the number one reason that people fail is that they do not have a clearly defined purpose.

According to countless media reports and publications, many people today feel their work lacks meaning and they are only working for a paycheck. These individuals often feel their lives are empty, and they feel unfilled. The essence of purpose, the inner spark that gives life meaning and fulfillment, is missing for them. Purpose is like an internal compass, guiding individuals and organizations. When it's missing, we feel lost.

Individual and organizational purposes are essential to each other. There is greater power to achieve and make things happen when aligned. The greater the convergence, the greater confidence individuals have that they are in the right place; for them, work is no longer a job to endure for a set number of hours each day. Instead, work allows them to express and realize their purpose in everyday action. These individuals often say they would do the work without pay! They are not clock-watchers; they work for the joy of doing something meaningful to them.

The two ovals in Figure 10 illustrate the Alignment of Organization and Employee Purposes. The top figure represents an employee working for a paycheck, with minimal shared purpose with the organization. By contrast, the other figure illustrates an alignment of purposes between the Organization and Employee.

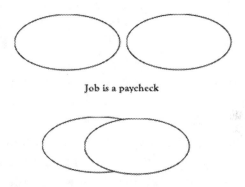

Job is a paycheck

The organization is a place to realize my purpose

Figure 11: Alignment of Organizational and Employee Purposes

Setting direction and developing a strategy to realize the organization's purpose and mission, vision and goals is the responsibility of senior leaders, while employees are responsible for implementing assigned decisions.

Employees often operate in a vacuum, are unfamiliar with

the organization's strategic plan, its purpose and mission. Some leaders assume it is unnecessary to communicate the organization's mission to employees nor engage them in recognizing how their work contributes to the mission, vision, and goals. They assume it is unnecessary because employees are paid for work, missing an opportunity to engage employees.

We will, however, recommend ways to engage employees in discovering how to contribute to the organization's mission and, in so doing, realize their purpose.

> *Just as your car runs more smoothly and*
> *requires less energy to go faster and farther*
> *when the wheels are in perfect alignment, you*
> *perform better when your thoughts, feelings,*
> *emotions, goals, and values are in balance.*

Brian Tracy

Employee engagement has become a significant issue in organizations. Recent estimates indicate that most employees are, at best, 30 to 40% productive. According to the Aberdeen Research Group, the good news is that when employees are engaged, they are more than 31% more productive. These statistics show us how vital engaging the human spirit is, which seeks meaning and purpose in life, a quest shared by people everywhere. Without meeting the need for meaning work, it is highly unlikely that employees will be motivated to work hard to achieve the organization's mission and goals.

There are numerous books to help people reflect on and focus their purpose, and there are even more books on developing an organizational purpose or mission. However, very few books address the importance of integrating organizational mission and individual purpose and including how to do this. This book is unique in that it addresses this critical gap.

Employees need an organizational context in which they can contribute to the organization's mission, and in so doing, realize their own purpose.

Individuals with a strong sense of purpose often have made significant contributions. Leaders keep purpose alive by finding ways to connect organizational and departmental purpose with their employees on an ongoing basis. When personal purpose aligns with that of the organization, they can also achieve significant results.

The challenge is connecting individual purpose with their role in the organization as an outlet for their purpose. If accomplished, the organization can allow employees to express their passion, talents, and the difference they want to make in the world.

Clarifying and Articulating Your Purpose

Long gone are the rites and rituals that connect people with their life purpose and the difference they are here to make. Some Indigenous tribes' elders foresaw the child's talents and future role in their communities. In many other cultures, it was traditional for children to follow in the vocational footsteps of their parents. In today's world, individuals must take responsibility for determining their purpose.

There are many ways for individuals to connect their head with their heart, focus on their lives. There is no one universal prescription for individuals to connect with their inner spirit and then live it in the world. Over a lifetime, our sense of purpose continues to evolve. We must discover what is most meaningful to us at different stages of our lives. Life presents us with different experiences from which we can reflect on the core questions of who we are, what gives us meaning, what our life purpose is and how we wish to live it out.

By recognizing that we alone are responsible for creating our lives, we can ask ourselves these questions:

- What makes me happy? What am I doing when I experience a great sense of satisfaction?
- What pain and suffering have I experienced or seen that I would like to address?
- About what do I care deeply?
- What kind of person do I want to be?
- What talents, skills, and abilities do I have to share with the world, and in what way?
- What gives meaning to me and for me?
- If I didn't need to earn a living, what would I love to do?
- What difference do I want to make with my life? How would I like to be remembered?
- What is my definition of success?

Although this is not an exhaustive list, these questions will stimulate thinking about personal purpose—they can start or expand your thinking. Consciously asking ourselves these types of reflective questions is vital to making sense of our lives and clarifying our purpose.

Tip: To get better answers, ask better questions.

Organizational Purpose

Just as purpose is vital for individuals, organizations need to have a core purpose and reason beyond making money. Money may result from meaningful action, but it is rarely an organization's primary purpose.

Founder(s) typically start a business recognizing a vital need or a purpose for creating the organization. After signing the James Bay Northern Quebec Agreement, Cree leaders recognized a need for a regional air link in the James Bay territory.

The territorial leaders knew if they didn't establish their airline, someone else would come into the area, fill the void, and seize the market.

Following the acquisition of a smaller airline, I worked with the combined management team of the regional airline. During the planning session, we developed the purpose of the expanded airline. Initially, it had been established to bring people in and out of the territory and transport goods, as the road system was minimal. In focusing the purpose statement for the newly constituted airline, the management team articulated the purpose:

> *Air Creebec is an air transportation company dedicated to be a vital air link, providing a safe, convenient and efficient service: being profitable enough to sustain long-term viability and to contribute to the Cree Nation's development.*

Fifteen years later that purpose statement is still true for the organization. In *Built to Last*, Collins and Porras state that purpose, the raison d'etre of an organization, is true forever. Although the wording might be adjusted or updated to reflect expanded consciousness, the core purpose remains true. "Mission," on the other hand, is short-term and focuses on a major goal or challenge, sometimes referred to as a BHAG—a Big Hairy Audacious Goal.

To illustrate the contrast, when NASA was established in the 1950s, its mission was to put a man on the moon, which it did successfully in August 1969. Once accomplished, NASA did not cease to operate because it had a larger purpose to explore space. The entire organization became re-energized and committed to fulfilling this updated larger purpose.

Typically, purpose and mission are integrated for expediency. These statements answer questions such as:

- Why do we exist - what is our primary purpose?
- Who are our customers?
- What services and products do we provide?
- What makes us unique or different?

Tewatohnhi'saktha Mission

The mission of Tewatohnhi'saktha is to stimulate and enhance Kahnawake's Economic Growth by investing in people and businesses, as well as other economic opportunities.

Mission of the Moose Cree First Nation

The mission of the Moose Cree First Nation is to support citizens to become self-sufficient. To achieve this, we provide services that foster and enhance physical, spiritual, emotional, and mental well-being. We sustain our culture and homeland within a dynamic and changing environment.

Figure 12: Examples—Mission Statements

Integrating Personal and Organizational Purpose/ Mission

Although an organization's purpose or mission does not typically change extensively, there are exceptions. The former president of Motorola anticipated the changes happening in the communications industry. He knew that for Motorola to continue to grow and prosper, the company had to focus on the industry's future rather than concentrate solely on where it was at that time. By moving Motorola out of the retail industry and into integrated chips and wireless communication, Galvin created a company that has not only survived but thrived in a highly competitive market.

Anticipating the impact of future trends on its purpose and how to adapt and refocus is essential.

There is value in reviewing your mission and core values when updating a strategic plan – it provides an opportunity to consider the relevancy of the organization's purpose. The review is an opportunity to remind leaders and employees of the organization's foundation, what it wants to be, and its direction for the future. This foundation is an essential touchstone for subsequent steps in the planning process.

Questions to link organizational and personal purpose:

- What do you see as your contribution to the purpose and mission of the organization?
- What is important to you in realizing the organization's purpose and mission?
- How does the organization's purpose and mission allow you to realize what is important to you as a person?

- What difference do you want to make with your life, and how does the purpose and mission of the organization align with that?
- To what extent do the organizational mission and your department provide an opportunity for you to express what has heart and meaning for you?

Collins and Porras use the image of the Yin Yang symbol to illustrate that organizations have a dual need—to preserve their culture and stimulate growth. Culture is preserved through its mission and core values. The dynamic of stimulating growth is created through developing an expansive future vision.

B. Crystallize Your Vision

Shared Vision of a Desired Future

A mission statement clarifies the purpose of an organization and should be "inspirational," anchoring an organization. On the other hand, a vision is "aspirational," drawing the organization forward like a guiding star.

Vision stimulates progress. "If an organization is to meet the challenges of a changing world, it must be prepared to change everything about itself except its basic beliefs as it moves forward." According to Thomas J. Watson Jr., founder of IBM, the only sacred cow in an organization should be its basic business philosophy.

Vision provides direction and magnetizes people toward a shared end state, answering the question, "Where do we want to be in five, ten, or twenty years, providing focus and direction. Without agreement on what success looks like or clarity about your purpose or mission, you won't be able to agree on the best way to get there.

A vision describes what success looks like in words or visuals. A vision is used primarily as a planning tool and not simply as a motivational tool.

> *The ability to imagine or have a vision is one of*
> *the key ingredients in making something happen.*

Ancient wisdom tells us people perish without vision which is valid for individuals and organizations. As a world-class museum volunteer, I heard a presentation by a city historian about historical city buildings and their use at that time. Most striking was the number of companies that no longer exist with only a short-term vision to provide a specific product or service. Similarly, Tom Peters followed up on the progress of "excellent companies" from his initial research for *In Search of Excellence*, discovering that less than 50% of those companies still existed.

Annette Redrick, former president of The Body Shop, said, "If you have an itsy-bitsy vision, you'll have an itsy-bitsy future." Not only is it vital for an organization to have a vision, but it is also essential to think big.

The Power of Visioning a New Future—the Nemaska Story

Some years ago, I had the opportunity to work with the Cree Nation of Nemaska, whose members were told that their village was about to be flooded. They had only a few hours to pack what they could carry and go to one of two other villages by plane. As a result, family groups became separated, and the people found themselves living in tents in the least desirable areas of the communities to which they had were transported.

Eventually, in a precedent-setting land claim, monies were set aside to re-establish a new community for the Nemaska Band. The land claim agreement stipulated that the band must re-establish a new community within five years.

KPMG, where I had been hired as a management consultant, had already been contracted to provide audit, accounting, and management consulting services to the Grand Council of the Crees of Quebec (GCCO). Given our existing relationship and knowledge of issues that the Nemaska people faced, I proposed to the Cree leaders and Chief of Nemaska that we hold a community consultation with the leaders and members of the Nemaska Band to create a plan to re-establish their community. At this point, the five-year clock was ticking and was already close to the four-year mark.

After accepting our planning proposal, we met with a core planning team of client members and our KPMG team to prepare for the five-day session. The planning session was held at Nemaska's members chosen site with approximately one hundred of their members, where we all tented for the week. Another consultant and I co-facilitated the five-day planning session. The Regional staff of the Cree Nation who spoke both Cree and English were trained and acted as the facilitators for the subgroup planning workshops with the members. In addition, another dozen stakeholders with specialized knowledge, such as architects, lawyers, engineers, and government officials, were on-site to provide information and advice as it was sought and needed during the planning session.

At the end of the planning session, held in a big-top style tent and five smaller tents for group work, the first step in the planning process had been accomplished—they had developed a plan for re-establishing their community. The community plan had a compelling and shared vision, which reflected the dreams and hopes of the Nemaska people— not just what advisors might have wanted. The plan was comprehensive, including six vision elements: education, health, social, economic development, and political skills development.

See figure 13 below, which depicts the Shared Vision Chart –Cree Nation of Nemaska.

The Cree Nation of Nemaska story is a powerful example of the fantastic results of forward-thinking, results-oriented, strategic planning and reflects change management principles.

Nemaska Consult – Practical Vision (September 1977)

Securing and Expanding the Economic Base		Building the Physical Base			Establishing the Community Base	
TRADITIONAL PURSUITS	**LOCAL ENTERPRISES**	**PHYSICAL FACILITIES**	**BASIC UTILITIES**	**SOCIAL SERVICES**	**SKILLS DEVELOPMENT**

Figure 13: Example–Practical Shared Vision Chart –Cree Nation of Nemaska

Twenty-five years later, I had the opportunity to work with the Chief and the community members to celebrate the community's progress towards its vision. In reviewing the plan, of the 125 specific vision elements in the six major vision categories, 100 had been completed. A number were still ongoing, e.g., reorganizing the trap lines. A couple of vision elements had been discarded, as they did not fit with the culture of the members. Another 25 new projects which had not been conceived originally had also been carried out.

*Legacies are built on visions that exceed
your ability to achieve them. Never limit
yourself to just what you think you can do.*

Author unknown

Conditions Necessary for Change

The Beckhard--Harris change model describes the conditions necessary for change to occur. The model specifies that organizations and individuals change when....

D – There is DISSATISFACTION with the current state (whatever the focus of change might be), and,

V – There is a clear and shared VISION (of a preferred future), and,

F – There are clear and productive FIRST STEPS, and

R – A Roadmap to achieving the vision.

The product of D x V x F is greater than the existing RESISTANCE to change among those whose support is required for successful implementation. These conditions give rise to a change formula: **D x V x F > R**

This change formula also implies that all three elements on

the left side, Desire, Vision, and First Steps must be present for change to occur. If any element is missing, the product of multiplication is zero, which will always be less than the Resistance to change, which is always present to some degree.

DISSATISFACTION with the status quo

All change begins with (a) dissatisfaction with the current state based on a recognition that the pain of not changing is likely to be greater than the uncertainty of change, and (b) a willingness to search for alternatives. The combination of these two elements creates a desire for change. Organizational leaders should never take for granted that the rest of the enterprise will see the need for change as clearly as they do (see "the Marathon effect, below).

A VISION for change

When individuals or groups desire change, but cannot identify a "way out," the result is anger, depression, frustration, anxiety and/or apathy. Whatever the reaction, it is seldom positive.

Mobilizing the energy generated by a desire for change requires a Vision. At its simplest, a shared vision is the answer to the question, "What do we want to create or achieve—together?"

First Steps

Although Dissatisfaction without Vision often leads to despair, Vision without Action is no more than a "castle in the air", a great idea without a roadmap. This can also create frustration and feelings of helplessness, resulting in apathy and or cynicism.

When engaging organizational members in the process of

change, they must have the opportunity to describe their own reality, influence the shaping of a new vision for the future, and participate in developing action plans (First Steps) for making the vision a reality.

RESISTANCE to change

In order that the product of Desire, Vision, and First Steps is greater than the Resistance to change, it is vital to gauge the degree and nature of resistance.

Organizations do not resist change — people do. And although they resist change for highly personal reasons, there are some general principles. People resist change when they...

- believe they will lose something of value in the change (status, belonging, competence)
- lack trust in those promoting or driving the change
- feel they have insufficient knowledge about the proposed change and its implications
- fear they will not be able to adapt to the change and will not have a place in the organization
- believe the change is not in the best interests of the organization
- believe they have been provided insufficient time to understand and commit to the change.

> *It's not that people resist change; it's just*
> *that they resist "being changed."*

Richard Beckhard

The most effective method of dealing with resistance is to engage stakeholders in shaping the elements on the left side of the change equation. By involving stakeholders in assessing the need for change (Dissatisfaction), co-creating a Vision of a preferred future, and determining First Steps toward the vision, the system not only becomes richer in wisdom and passion, it defuses many real or potential concerns about the change.

I have adapted Beckhard's change model: D/DVAPL = C

Dissatisfaction/ Desire > *Vision* + *Action* +
Leadership + *Persistence* = **CHANGE**

Dissatisfaction must be turned into Desire and crystalized in a Vision. Action must be taken to realize the vision. Leadership is needed to guide and encourage. Persistence is needed to persevere to realize results and achieve Change.

To illustrate: The Nemaska people were dissatisfied with their current situation; dissatisfied with being divided, living in the worst areas of their temporary communities, and having the last opportunities for employment in these communities, were just some of the issues they faced. They were dissatisfied enough to want to bring about change, and they desired something better for themselves and their children.

The community planning consultation process allowed the Nemaska members to focus their desire for something better into a powerful, compelling shared vision. For example, one of the vision elements was for simple log homes like they had in the" bush" or out on the land. Another vision element was to build the community with trees around the housing clusters, rather than bulldozing them for practicality, as had been done in many other communities. When I facilitated the 25th year celebration in the community, one modest log home was still in place, and the housing clusters was nestled in clumps of trees, reflecting the northern way of life.

In developing their plan, members had considered obstacles blocking them from realizing their vision. Rather than let the obstacles defeat them, they developed strategies and actions to unblock their desired future.

Having a plan and realizing it is another matter. The Chief provided persistent leadership implementing the plan day-after-day, year-after-year. He stayed the course and saw the plan through to completion, without which the plan would not have been implemented.

Many great plans are developed every day. Some leaders abandon the plan in favor of a "shiny new object." The goal of such leaders is often to have a planning session and claim to have a plan, *not* to implement it. Leadership commitment is essential to successfully develop and implement plans and follow through in realizing results.

A few years after the 25th-anniversary celebration, I was working in my office one morning when the phone rang. It was Chief Wapachee from Nemaska. He announced, "We did it, we did the last one!" I was puzzled momentarily, not knowing what he was talking about. I asked, "The last what?" He said, "The last vision element." Being curious, I asked, "What was it?" Chief Wapachee told me, "The Bible Camp," which had been built that summer. How appropriate it was, I thought, to complete the community plan in a way that expresses gratitude to God for their progress and what they had achieved.

A powerful vision gives hope for the future. Viktor Frankl in his book, *Man's Search for Meaning*, tells how vital vision was for prisoners in the Nazi concentration camps to stay alive. He held in his imagination the vision of being at Carnegie Hall in New York City, giving a lecture. He also tells how once other prisoners who had no vision, they gave up, died within days.

In my early twenties, I had the opportunity to visit the Buchardt Gardens in Victoria, BC. I recall looking at the gardens and thinking that they were nice. Twenty years later, I revisited the gardens and saw them through a different set of eyes. I had a new appreciation for the magnificent beauty, vibrant colors, and design of the gardens.

I was in awe of Mrs. Buchard vision to create a spectacular garden from a gutted-out limestone quarry to a sunken garden section. The story says when all the limestones had been extracted, Mrs. Buchardt announced her vision to create a beautiful garden in the gutted quarry. I can only imagine how the workmen laughed, thinking this woman to be a bit mad, a beautiful garden in the ugly quarry? Despite its appearance, Mrs. Buchardt held fast to her vision. She was let down in a basket to insert plantings in the side of the quarry walls. Over time her magnificent vision took on form and grandeur.

Many other examples of vision exist and are common knowledge. One such story is of the Israelites, whose vision was to get to the "promised land." It took 40 years of marching through the desert to turn their vision into reality, and they never gave up.

The lesson we can learn from these examples is that accomplishing a vision for something better requires the passion and commitment of all stakeholders.

Guidelines for Visions: A vision needs to:

- reflect what the planning group members care about most deeply and genuinely want to create;
- be a shared creation. In other words, the vision should be co-created by the planning team members, which could include the management team, or council, or board of directors;
- be stated in the present tense as if it is a reality, see Figure 13;
- be stated in the positive so that it becomes a focus of what you want to move toward, acting as a guiding star; and
- be compelling, pointing to a future that is better than what exists today.

Creating a Powerful Vision

Recently I worked with the board of directors and management team of an organization wanting to develop a strategic plan.

When we began the process, I noticed writing tablets on the tables that had the names of the divisions of the organization with the statement, "One Vision." I was fascinated and asked, "What is the vision?"

Although they did not yet have One vision, there was an understanding that one was needed.

During the planning session, we created a shared vision for the organization. We used a powerful process in which individuals were taken on a guided visualization into the future for the organization. Following the visualization, each person jotted down their images and impressions of the future using words or drawings. In small groups, participants shared three to five of their visionary ideas that they most wanted to see, hear, or have. In the process of sharing, they discovered similarities and some differences.

Each sub-group then selected a given number of vision elements that they collectively wanted to see in the overall vision. The next step was to gather, organize and cluster similar visionary ideas from the subgroups.

Following this, divergent ideas were added, expanding the vision clusters. After all vision elements had been arranged in groupings pointing to the same theme, we reviewed each vision cluster, asking ourselves what the vision each grouping pointed to. Having named each vision cluster, the planning team came up with an overall, integrated vision statement of what they wanted to see and where they wanted their organization to be in the next five to ten years. It is tempting to want to get the wording perfect, and it is important not to get hung up on word-smithing the vision — instead, focus on capturing its essence.

When a vision comes together, people typically get very excited. It is like the fog lifts, and a beautiful scene unfolds before them.

The Workshop Method Visioning Process described above, was developed at the Institute of Cultural Affairs (ICA) after many years of experimenting and fine-tuning with communities and organizations worldwide. What is powerful about the ICA process is that it produces a holistic, multi-faceted vision.

Sometimes a vision is stated in one or two sentences to summarize the more significant, richly imagined ideal future, such as in the vision statements below:

Tewatohnhi'saktha Vision

Tewatohnhi'saktha contributes to developing a self-sufficient community that fosters quality of life for Kanien'kehaka Ne Kahnawa'kehró:non and creates collective prosperity for future generations consistent with our cultural values.

Vision of the Moose Cree First Nation

We are a sovereign nation with a sustainable local economy. We have a strong evolving Ililew culture in which we speak our language and live our traditions day-to-day. Our citizens are educated in both traditional and contemporary knowledge. Our people are healthy, educated, self-sufficient, and have strong families. Moose Cree citizens actively participate in decision-making.

Figure 14: Examples of Vision Statements

In addition to the ICA visioning process, there are other visioning processes. If time is restricted, a shorter exercise is to have a group imagine that a leading magazine or TV that they respect has produced a feature article about their organization or nation, then ask the group to describe what the story says about their organization or nation.

Visions that are genuinely shared require ongoing conversation, and a vision is rarely neatly wrapped up during a planning process. Often, some further discussion is required to polish the vision statement—just like polishing a gem to bring out all its facets and brilliance.

Remember that vision is a living creation—it exists in language or representation. To keep the vision alive, you need to talk about it and review it frequently. As you talk about your vision, it will become clearer, sharpening your sense of the primary elements of your vision and keeping your people inspired and engaged.

C. Articulate Core Values

What are Core Values

In addition to aligning personal and organizational purpose/ mission; having a shared, compelling vision, organizations need to have a set of shared core values to guide how they work together in accomplishing their mission and vision. Core values also articulate how the organization treats customers, suppliers, and everyone it encounters.

Values are the glue that holds the culture of an organization together. We often hear that there is little difference between the products and services of organizations. Yet, how its products and services are delivered reflects the core values of that organization.

Therefore, an organization needs to consider the core values lived daily. What do they mean to the organization? How do you live them? Remember that core values may not get identified in the first year of developing a strategic plan.

Defining the organization's core values can be done as a particular project, allowing everyone time to consider what they are, reflecting how an organization does things, differentiating it from other organizations. For each core value, it is essential to identify the specific behaviors that serve as indicators to ensure employees understand what it means to live them daily.

Marcelene Anderson

Guidelines for Developing Core Values

Collins and Porras suggest that you should *not* ask, "What core values *should* we hold?"

Instead, ask: "What core values *do we hold*, not just espouse?" Core values and purpose must be passionately held at a gut level or are not core.

Values you think the organization "ought" to have but cannot honestly say that it does have should not be mixed into the authentic core values. Doing so creates cynicism throughout the organization.

I recently advised a client group working to identify the actual core values of their organization to identify their actual core beliefs about how people act and treat each other. After brainstorming what they perceived were the most important behaviors that define the organization, we clustered the behaviors into major categories, grouping similar ones, eliminating duplications, and refining the list. Next, we chose those values that were of most importance or core to the organization.

We accomplished this by giving each participant a set number of votes to identify their choices from the list of possible values. The values that received the highest number of votes were identified to be core. As a group, we agreed on a manageable number of core values, e.g., five to seven. Too many would be forgotten, while too few would be insufficient and not adequately reflect the organization's most important values.

The wording of each core value was fine-tuned, making the meaning clearer and ensuring that it reflected the way the organization intended it. We then identified the behaviors we would expect to see if someone exhibited those values.

Specific behaviors for each core value were identified and refined, honing them to reflect expected behaviors and integrated into their performance management system. Additionally, the core values were integrated into the strategic plan providing a framework for realizing its mission and vision.

Core values have a sense of timelessness. In the mid-nineties, I assisted a community in developing a strategic plan. Several years later we updated the strategic plan, we reviewed their values. It was amazing to discover how timeless the value statements were and essential in how members and employees interact and work together.

Tewatohnhi'saktha Values

Values reflect who we are and what we continuously strive to become. At Tewatohnhi'saktha, we strive to be:

- Results-Oriented
- Accountable
- Progressive and Innovative
- Professional
- Customer Focused
- Employee Focused
- Teamwork Oriented
- Open and Honest

Figure 15: Examples of Values Statements Tewathnhi'saktha

Core Value #1 Results-Oriented

Being results-oriented is a core element of the Tewatohnhi'saktha culture that supports our reason for being and provides credible, recognizable, and significant evidence to all our stakeholders and ourselves.

Results-Oriented means:

- Ensuring our daily, weekly, and monthly actions are planned towards meeting pre-determined goals and objectives, which are flexible to changing demands and new priorities.
- Setting key measures of success for short, medium, and long-term goals and objectives while ensuring alignment with the vision and mission.
- Creating strategies that are well thought out, supportive and effective to achieving the desired ends.
- Investing and deploying the required resources to ensure success
- Continuously striving to produce excellent results
- Regularly evaluating progress, acknowledging our mistakes, and learning from them, so that we can do better next time

Used with permission of Tewatohnhi'saktha.
All rights reserved.

Moose Cree First Nation Values

Another example of an organization that created a set of values is the Moose Cree First Nation.

Moose Cree First Nation

Values reflect who we are and what we continuously strive to become. At Moose Cree First Nation, we strive for:

• Understanding	• Love
• Spirituality	• Learning
• Respect	• Communication
• Family	• Responsibility

Figure 16: Example: Values Statement Moose Cree First Nation

Responsibility means:

We believe that we are here to fulfill a responsibility to our children, our families, and ourselves. We will strive to achieve our full potential now and for future generations.

Respect means:

We believe by working together, we can build a caring community, by accepting others whose opinions and ideas are valued.

Used with permission of Moose Cree First Nation. All rights reserved.

As a consultant, I see, hear, and feel the differences in values among various organizations with whom I work. When values are core, day-to-day behaviors are the same as those on paper, and they are not just nice-sounding words on a plaque but genuinely reflect the organization's culture. Core values are like oil to an engine, helping the parts to operate efficiently, just as they make day-to-day operations of an organization function smoothly.

Developing Core Values

- Consider and brainstorm what employees believe to be the core values of behaving and treating each other and clients/citizens.
- Consider what makes working in the organization different than others—what does this organization value?
- What makes it different?

> *The primary purpose of values is to guide our actions and our decisions. 'Words to live by' are just words... unless you live by them.*

Eric Harvey

Getting clear on your desired future is a starting point for creating your desired future.

> *You never change something by fighting the existing reality. To change something, build a new model that makes the existing model obsolete.*

Buckminster Fuller

D. Create Your Rallying Cry

The rallying cry should be a crisp, motivational slogan of several words, 3-6, easily remembered by all organizational members, such as Ford Corp.s, 'Quality is Job One.'

Be sure it is a powerful, motivating expression for your staff that is inspirational, believable, and repeatable daily in your organization.

To develop a rallying cry, you will first need to define your organization's primary driving force within your mission, and vision statements, together called your Strategic Intent. One of my clients, an economic development organization intent was to accelerate its results contributing to the economic self-sufficiency of its nation. They choose '*Climbing Mt. Everest*' as they recognized it was going to be a challenging and steep undertaking.

A holding company had a rallying cry, '*One Vision*', for all the subsidiary companies. Although they had not yet created it, which we developed together, they understood they needed just one vision and then created it.

The rallying cry is a concept:

- Taken from or builds on the mission, vision, and values statements (why)
- That expresses what makes you unique from other organizations
- Comprises the *whos*, *whats*, and *hows*, or assumes them in the statement
- The basis for making decisions and criteria
- It cannot be readily duplicated
- Is unique to the organization
- Reflects your current reality or can become one within planning timeframe.

Your rallying cry is not a marketing slogan and should be used consistently throughout your operations as an underlying basis for making decisions. It will motivate staff, reminding them of your vision statement. As such, it should be memorable, meaningful, believable, and be able to be repeated daily.

Examples:

- McDonald's: *Quality Service, Cleanliness (QSC)*
- Disney: *We create happiness*
- Ford: *Quality is Job One*
- Canadian Standards Association: *Making Our Mark on the World*

Tip

To avoid your rallying cry from being hokey and unnecessary, wait until the end of the strategic planning session to develop your rallying cry. Actively involve members of your organization through an organization-wide contest for the best rallying cry.

First, you must make them aware of your organization's strategic plan, e.g., its mission, vision, and values; then, ask them to submit their ideas which helps them create a sense of ownership for the organization and implementation of the plan. Then, have top management publicly announce the winning phrase, and reward those who have submitted it.

Chapter 6: Step: 3: Measuring Results

What gets measured gets done

Without keeping score, it is not a game. Similarly, without measuring progress toward your desired future (mission, vision, and values), employees are less likely to be in the game, accountable for results, and an organization is less likely to reach its desired future.

Many planning processes leap from visioning to objective setting without measuring progress towards the mission and vision.

A few years ago, I met a leader of an organization, which had just completed developing a strategic plan. They engaged my services to assist them in carrying out an employee satisfaction survey. Following the survey, I inquired if they had a systematic process for implementing their strategic plan, and they replied that they did not but were interested in one.

We had a dynamic kick-off launch event to begin the implementation process. All the senior managers presented their objectives for the next three years, outlining what they planned to do year-one and quarter-one. Everyone was excited with high energy, everyone knew what they had to do. With this focus, they began to execute their plans.

A few months later, we came back together to report on progress toward the plan. As each senior manager said what had done over the past quarter, each of us listened attentively. While listening, I had an image in my mind of them climbing a mountain in a blinding snowstorm; although they were furiously climbing, we could not tell if they were making progress or just going around in circles. Something was missing.

After the session, the CEO and I resolved that later in the year, when the strategic plan was to be updated, we would develop and put in place a system to measure progress toward the desired future.

Benefits of Measuring Progress

Measuring progress is essential for many reasons. The reality is that most of us get caught up in the day-to-day chaos of activities that seem necessary, making it easy to lose focus on those things that are genuinely critical to achieving our objectives.

Establishing key performance measures helps us keep our eye on the most vital activities to continue to drive progress toward achieving goals. Measuring progress allows us to choose where to focus our energy daily to progress towards our desired future.

Another reason for measuring progress is to give employees a way to know that their efforts make a meaningful difference. Engaging them in creating their scorecard and measuring progress, they are motivated and focused on those key activities that produce results. Another reason for measuring progress is that they have increased awareness of the impact of their actions on achieving goals.

Balanced Scorecards

One of the most critical elements to achieving results is establishing a holistic set of key performance measures to monitor progress toward the organization's mission, vision, and values. Harvard professors Kaplan and Norton popularized the concept of a Balanced Scorecard in 1992 based on a holistic set of measures. One of the primary benefits of balanced scorecards, or dashboards, is better alignment of long-term strategies with short activities.

A balanced scorecard is a strategic measurement-based system that translates its organization's mission and vision statement into specific, measurable targets or goals and measures performance toward them.

Balanced scorecards go beyond the traditional indicators, such as financial performance, and help measure employee performance and satisfaction, customer satisfaction, and operational efficiency. One of the primary benefits of balanced scorecards is better alignment of long-term strategies with short activities.

Most organizations are already measuring some or all these four areas. Typically, data about performance is in departmental and employee files.

One of the benefits of an organizational scorecard is that all the critical organizational key success measures and indicators are in one shared organizational electronic system and paper files, making it more accessible.

Developing Your Scorecard

To develop a Scorecard, an organization or a department reviews its mission, vision, and values asking, "What are the most vital areas of our mission, vision, and values toward which we should measure progress?" Once the Key Success Areas are defined, the next step is to decide how to measure each by selecting Performance Indicators. For example, you measure employee engagement by the percentage of satisfied employees. Unless the organization already has existing data on employee satisfaction, you can assess it through a survey.

Other indicators frequently chosen to measure employee satisfaction are the number of days employees are absent, employee turnover rate, and retention. Customer satisfaction can be measured by the percentage of satisfied customers and retention year-over-year. Financial indicators might include gross revenue, sales, profitability, and stakeholder satisfaction, e.g., the percentage of satisfied stakeholders.

Measuring performance is one of the best practices of high-performing organizations—*what gets measured gets managed and done.*

In a recent client meeting where the goal was to update the strategic plan, we discussed the amount of time and effort required and its cost benefits. The CEO reminded the team that having targets had significantly impacted their progress. "Although the process is not perfect," he told them, "measuring progress had increased the level of results achieved compared to when we did strategic planning based only on goals and objectives."

The process of setting Key Success Areas, Performance Indicators, and targets had clarified expectations and what was necessary.

Without performance measures or targets, measuring progress systematically, organizations often make little or no progress.

Moreover, if employees do not recognize a gap between expectations and current results, they are less compelled to make continuous improvements towards higher performance levels.

Once an organization has established its Performance Indicators, the next step is to set targets for a pre-determined period, typically three to five years. In my experience, three years is preferable as it is a more manageable period. Five-year targets can be more difficult to establish because too many unknown variables that could affect targets.

Identifying key success areas, developing key performance indicators, and setting targets for each are the most challenging aspects of establishing your feedback system. This is an area where an organization can make a quantum leap in its results.

The first year is typically the most challenging for an organization as it considers the most vital areas of its mission and vision and decides how to measure progress by choosing performance indicators for each. For example, while a survey might be desirable to carry out each year, the time and costs incurred may be prohibitive. As a result, the organization may conduct a major survey only once during a planning cycle and do mini or pulse surveys annually to monitor progress.

Creating Your Scorecard or Dashboard

A popular concept for tracking results is called a 'scorecard' or a 'dashboard'. Creating an organizational dashboard or scorecard requires a new way of measuring progress towards your desired future. Most of us do not monitor all dashboard gauges in our vehicles, and we pay attention to only a critical few.

Creating your dashboard or scorecard requires selecting the keywords or phrases from the mission and vision representing success, e.g., economic growth. For the chosen Key Success Areas, choose Performance. Indicators to measure it, e.g., you can measure economic growth by the number of joint ventures. Set 3-year target for each Performance Indicator. See the example below:

Vision:
Enhance economic growth by investing in people, businesses, and other financial opportunities.

Key Success Areas:
- Capacity building
- New business growth
- Business expansion
- Revenue generation

Performance Indicators for Business Expansion:
- Joint ventures
- Expansion into new markets

3 Year Targets
- # of business start-ups
- # of business expansions
- % of repeat clients

Setting Targets
- For each key performance indicator, what is our current level of performance, which will serve as the benchmark for setting three-year targets?
- If no data currently exists, establish benchmark data through a survey or a study during the current year.

- Current data can be used to establish targets for the last year of the planning cycle.
- Considerations for establishing three-year targets:
  - Previous levels of achievement
  - The new needed level of results
  - Resources required to achieve them (internal and external)

Once three-year targets have been established, you can then work backward to the level of attainment wanted for year two and year one to realize the three-year cumulative targets.

Lead and Lag Targets

Organizations need a reporting process to ensure the correct information is provided at the right time to make critical decisions. To increase the likelihood, your goal will be accomplished, create several measures, some 'Lead' and 'some Lag' Indicators. Bodyweight, for example, is a lag measure because it is a result of choices made during the day. The lead measures are the number of calories consumed through eating and the number burned through activity. Tracking exercise is a lead indicator that promotes habits needed to reach and maintain health and weight goals, a lag indicator. In business, sales volume is also a lag indicator because it results from other activities.

A good lead measure is actionable and allows you to influence future results and not just measure them after the fact. For example, while you can measure rainfall and even predict the amount of rain, you cannot influence how much precipitation will fall, and rainfall is not a lead measure.

On the other hand, focusing on reducing equipment failures (a simple lead measure), one organization significantly increased output (a lag measure). Sales lead indicators are the number of qualified prospects in a sales funnel, promotional times sent out, or appointments.

Lag indicators help us work backward through the problem/ situation. Instead of becoming de-motivated, we work through the issues until we find the appropriate actions or behaviors to help us achieve lag measures.

Systems that help you focus on lead and lag indicators are helpful, allowing you to keep your eye on the primary target and the essential parts that influence it.

The closer you process inputs and activities, the closer you get to Leading Indicators of downstream (Lagging) performance. If you measure aggregated outcomes at an organizational level, you are more likely to be using Lagging Indicators.

Collecting current performance data and organizing it in one location is a significant challenge because it is typically scattered across many departments. An organization needs a dashboard that integrates all key success measures of an organization in one place is needed.

Creating Your Scorecard or Dashboard

Ownership by its users is vital in creating your departmental scorecards or dashboards. They need to decide how best to display their key success measures and targets to depict what is to be measured so that it is meaningful to them.

Many online dashboards or scorecard systems are available to customize for your organization. These systems allow employees at all levels to enter their data, and specified individuals have access to the information they need. An alternative and straightforward process can initially be developed using a software program such as Excel to report monthly, quarterly, and yearly.

A word of caution: Organizations often measure everything, which can be time-consuming. Therefore, in the second year of the plan, we recommend that an organization review and evaluate its key performance indicators to ensure the measurement system for measuring progress and updating its targets for the following year. See Figure 17, below. Questions that help to guide you in this process include:

- What are the most critical areas of our mission, vision, and values to measure?
- Based on past targets indicated in the baseline, are the targets too easy or challenging to meet based on our past results?

Organizational Dashboard Key Success Measures and Performance Indicators						
Key Success Measures and Performance Indicators	Baseline (Current Year)	Yearly Targets			3-Year Target	Responsibility
		Year 1	Year 2	Year 3		
EMPLOYEE SATISFACTION - Employee Satisfaction - Employee Retention						
CUSTOMER SATISFACTION - Customer Satisfaction - Customer Retention						
FINANCIAL VIABILITY - Revenue - Profitability						
BUSINESS GROWTH - Partnerships / Sub-contracts - Joint Ventures						
STAKEHOLDER SATISFACTION - Stakeholder knowledge of services						
STRATEGIC MANAGEMENT - Quarterly Review Meetings - Management Team Meetings - Review & Update SP						

Figure 17: Organizational Dashboard Key Success Areas & Performance Indicators Table

The combined Dashboard or Scorecard will help you know if your organization is on track, allowing you to identify areas where continuous improvements are needed. In the first year or two of implementing a Scorecard, some adjustments and refinements of the Key Performance Indicators are typically required.

The key questions to consider are: Are we measuring the right things? Will this tell us if we have made progress towards our desired future (our mission and vision)?

You are dealing with two new inter-related variables, managing for results or 'Ends' (key performance indicator targets) versus 'Means' or activities to accomplish the Ends. Driving for results instead of activities is a significant and critical shift for most organizations.

To assist you with monitoring performance and reporting, you may wish to use software which makes it easier to monitor progress for the whole organization as well as by department, and employees. Additionally, you can monitor the progress for a core strategy or strategic action initiatives.

By getting the suitable measures in place, monitoring, and discussing progress regularly, you will increase performance and results exponentially.

Summary

Remember, the overall purpose of establishing metrics is to track performance towards your goals. Develop and work with metrics that will drive you towards your ultimate goals.

*The greater danger for most of us is not
that our aim is too high, and we miss it,
but that it is too low, and we reach it.*

Author unknown

Chapter 7: Step 4: Assessing Your Current Situation

The gap between where you want to be and where you are

"*Your present circumstances don't determine where you can go; they merely determine where you start.*"

~Nido Qubein

Once an organization has a clear picture of where it wants to be in the future, and there is a system in place to measure progress toward it, the next step is to size up the gap between the desired future and the current situation, as well as to identify the obstacles that are blocking it.

Figure 18: Assess the Gap Between the Current and Desired Future

An excellent job of identifying the gaps and obstacles allows a planning group to identify the actions needed to get unblocked and move forward towards its desired future and results.

*Sensible decisions take into consideration
the world as it and will be.*

Isaac Asimov

Identifying the Gaps

The gap question can be asked in several ways, such as:

- What are the key gaps between where we want to be (our vision) and where we are today?
- How close are we to our desired future and the level of results we want to attain?
- How would we describe or characterize our current situation in each aspect of our vision?

Employees are often skeptical about mission and vision statements saying, "We are the best!" They know that it is not yet true. While it is vital to communicate that you *aspire* to be the best, it is prudent to do a reality check to determine where you are, assessing the gap between the desired future state and the actual current situation. Be honest and objective about where things stand, and make sure you communicate this to your employees to avoid the appearance that you are out of touch with reality.

Tap your team's perspective and invite them to identify the gaps and obstacles as well as the actions needed to close them. Acknowledging that there is room for improvement will increase employees' sense of credibility in the planning process. Engaging employees in finding solutions to close the gaps increases their sense of ownership for solutions and actions to bring about change.

Tip: Consider your best friends as skeptics who help you see past your blind spots. - Stephen Haines

---

When the desired future vision is clear and the team is engaged, planning team members can intuitively and openly discuss the gaps and propose the actions needed. In a planning session with the board of directors and management team of the holding company described in Chapter 4, once they were clear and excited about their vision, they were unstoppable in pointing out gaps and obstacles and proposing actions that were needed to close the gaps. The process of assessing the gaps and allowing new answers to emerge is vital for new ideas and actions to emerge, leading to better results.

We are all presented with opportunity, only a few take advantage of it.

Richard Branson

The Current State Assessment, shown in Figure 19, depicts a SWOT analysis process and template for assessing the current state to identify the gaps and obstacles to your desired future.

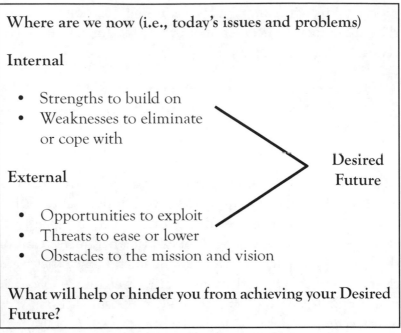

Where are we now (i.e., today's issues and problems)

Internal

- Strengths to build on
- Weaknesses to eliminate or cope with

External

- Opportunities to exploit
- Threats to ease or lower
- Obstacles to the mission and vision

What will help or hinder you from achieving your Desired Future?

Desired Future

Figure 19: Current State Assessment Process

In conducting a SWOT analysis, ask future-oriented questions and use the analysis to determine what actions to take.

Strengths
- What internal strengths do we have as an organization or department that we can use to realize our desired future?
- What actions might we take to build on our strengths to move closer to our desired future and results?

Weaknesses
- What internal weaknesses do we have as an organization or department that could limit or reduce the likelihood of realizing our desired future?

- What actions might we take to reduce our weaknesses to move closer to our desired future and results?

Opportunities

- What external opportunities do we have as an organization or department (from our Environmental Scan) that we can seize on to realize our desired future?
- What actions might we take to seize our opportunities and move closer to our desired future and results?

Threats

- What external threats do we face as an organization or department (from our Environmental Scan) that we need to prepare for and develop strategies to realize our desired future?
- What actions might we take to reduce the threats and move closer to our desired future and results?

Your organization may also carry out other specialized studies or review processes, such as an employee satisfaction survey or a customer satisfaction survey. Use these in conjunction with analyzing your organization's strengths and weaknesses in the SWOT analysis. In addition, the Environmental Scan provides a wealth of information about opportunities and threats.

Identifying the key gaps and obstacles to moving your organization to your desired future is vital in the planning process. Avoid the temptation to name a gap or an obstacle as something is missing—state what exists, e.g., unknown funding sources.

The bigger the challenge requires looking deeper at what is missing to understand what is creating "the absence of money." For example, it could be that there is insufficient business development or limited funding sources.

Push past the surface obstacles to look deeper at what is going on to increase your awareness of how the organization may be participating in creating the current situation.

Doing so allows you to consider new and different actions to move your organization toward its desired future.

If you can find a path with no obstacles,
it probably doesn't lead anywhere.

Frank A. Clark

Current State Assessment Summary

Summary	Actions
Strengths to build on • • •	**Actions** to build on Strengths • • •
Weakness to minimize • • •	**Actions** to minimize Weaknesses • • •
Opportunities to seize • • •	**Actions** to seize Opportunities • • •
Threats to reduce • • •	**Actions** to reduce Threats • • •
Obstacles to circumvent • • •	**Actions** to circumvent Obstacles • • •
Key Gaps between Desired Future and Current Situation • • •	

Figure 20: Current State Assessment Summary

The Current State Assessment helps you achieve a shared conscious perspective of the obstacles blocking your future and the critical gaps between your desired future and where you are today. This requires both analytical and creative thinking, leading to new actions that close the gaps and allow you to move past the obstacles.

As mentioned earlier, Albert Einstein said that insanity is doing the same thing repeatedly while expecting different results. The Current State Assessment helps you break out of that trap.

Summary

One of the significant values of identifying the strengths, weaknesses, opportunities, and threats is identifying specific actions to close the gaps between where you want to be and where you are currently, thereby moving you toward your desired future. These actions will be the foundation for developing your Core Strategies.

"What makes a plan strategic is that it's core strategies and its strategic actions close the gaps and move you towards your desired future."

Marcelene Anderson

Chapter 8: Step 5:
Strategies Development

Strategies to close gaps

In your analysis of the Current Situation, you have laid the groundwork for developing Core Strategies. You have begun to identify the actions needed to close gaps, navigate around or reduce obstacles, progress towards your mission & vision, and achieve your key success measure targets. Throughout the current state process, you have been determining the actions to be taken but have not yet narrowed down the options to choose the ideas or actions that would be best to employ.

Figure 21: Develop Strategies to Close the Gap

Strategies are the primary means to achieving your desired future and key success measures. They are the major methods or the how-to's.

Strategies are groups of related actions that, collectively, have a greater impact than a single action done on its own. Sometimes strategies are referred to as "objectives." Focus your energy by limiting your strategies to three to seven, which encompass several smaller actions which, when done collectively, increase the velocity and impact of the Core Strategy.

Tip: Strategies keep you focused on what is most important to do and keep you from doing nonessentials.

Strategies should be focused and directed to accomplish a specific aim. If you can implement the strategies in most departments, they are "Core Strategies" to achieve desired future results.

Developing Strategies

Building on the actions identified in the previous chapter, ask yourself, "What are the five to seven major actions that your organization should take to achieve the desired results and future."

Developing Core Strategies

- Identify what you consider to be the major actions needed to close the gaps and move your organization forward. Select five to seven major strategies.
- For each strategy, develop a descriptive title, e.g., "Strengthen Relationships with Key Stakeholders." The title should include a powerful verb and noun.
- Develop a one-sentence statement of intent for each strategy. See examples, below.

See below, Figure 22 which illustrates Core Strategies and Statement of Intent.

MCFN Core Strategies and Intent of Each

1. Enhance Communication At All Levels
To improve the flow of communication between all levels and with citizens.

2. Strengthen MCFN Governance
To prepare for effective, responsible, and accountable governance.

3. Enhance Employee Satisfaction
To create employment conditions to attract and retain employees that contribute to the success of the MCFN.

4. Prepare Moose Cree Citizens for Employment
To provide training and professional development for Moose Cree citizens to take advantage of current and future employment opportunities.

5. Develop a Sustainable MCFN Economy
To develop a sustainable Moose Cree economy that fosters self-reliant citizens.

6. Increase the Effectiveness of the Organizational Structure And Systems
To improve how we are structured and organized to meet the current and future needs of Moose Cree First Nation citizens.

7. Preserve the 'Ililew' Culture
To revitalize and sustain Ililew identity.

8. Enhance The Effectiveness Of Programs, Services and Infrastructure
To upgrade programs, services infrastructures to meet current and future MCFN citizen needs.

9. Implement the Strategic Management System
To successfully implement our strategic plan, monitor progress towards expected results, and keep our plan updated.

Figure 22: Examples–Core Strategies and Statement of Intent
Used with permission of the Moose Cree First Nation

Although many organizations list their strategies like those in the example above, the Cree Nation of Chisasibi was creative in depicting their strategies as a tepee, a culturally appropriate image. The eight-core strategies represent the poles of a tepee upholding the center, their values, traditions, and culture, see Figure 23, see below.

Figure 23: Circular Strategies Model

Things to Consider:

- Test to ensure the core strategies are likely to close the gaps and eliminate or reduce the obstacles identified in the Current Situation Assessment. Fine-tune your strategies, as necessary.
- The planning team must agree on the strategies and the intent of each.
- Most importantly, test if the core strategies will close the identified gaps and help you to bring about the

strategic difference you are seeking to move the organization closer to its desired future.

- Test to see that the strategies are "Core," meaning most of your business units or departments would be able to implement them. If the strategies do not apply to most departments, they are likely strategic actions to be included only in departmental plans.

Developing Strategic Actions Initiative to implement the Core Strategies

Once the planning team agrees on the Core Strategies and the intent of each, you are ready to determine the actions needed to implement each Core Strategy.

To do this, describe the paradigm shift needed to implement the strategy and realize its intent. A paradigm is a way we see the world that is producing the current results. For many decades, an accepted paradigm was that the world was flat. As we now know, new data allowed people to update or shift their paradigm about the shape of the world.

To determine what actions are needed to move the organization toward its target year goals, complete the following steps:

- Draw a T-bar across the top of a page, extending about a quarter of the way down the page to create two columns (see Figures 24 and Example 25), adapted from the Systems Thinking Approach to Strategic Management).
- Title the left-hand column with the current year; describe in point form the actual way things are in the present, including the positives, negatives, and

other descriptions about the current situation for this strategy.

- In the right-hand column, identify the end year of the current planning cycle (i.e., three years into the future) and use it as the title for this column. Describe in point form what you would like to see or have in place by that year.
- List the actions needed to move your organization toward what you want by the end of the current planning cycle, e.g., the next three or more years.
- Select the six to nine actions that you regard as the most strategic to shift from the current state to the end of the planning cycle.
- Refine the description of the core strategy situation and possible actions.
- Remember that each core strategy needs a set of strategic action initiatives over the planning horizon, e.g., the next three or more years.
- These are the activities and actions required over the planning cycle to realize each Core Strategy.
- Make a final review of the proposed actions and agree on the best strategic action initiatives to realize the paradigm shift over the current planning cycle.

*Great things are not done by impulse, but by
a series of small things brought together.*

Vincent van Gogh (1853–1890)

Marcelene Anderson

Core Strategy #_____

Intent:

Today:	Target Year:
*	*
*	*
*	*

Figure 24: *Core Strategies Development Worksheet*

Core Strategy #2
Expand CREECO Businesses

Intent: Identify and seize the best business opportunities.

2009	2012
• Stable operations with relatively low level of expansion • 3 of 4 CREECO businesses are same as when CREECO was established • Primary focus has been within the Cree Territory	• Reduce Lost workdays from accidents reduced by 25% • More diversity in company • Enter new markets (also geographical)

Strategic Action Items:

	2009-2010	2010-2011	2011-2012
Develop working relationships with EDO's, local development corporations, and entrepreneurs	√	√	
Establish partnerships and joint ventures	√		
Pursue Joint ventures in specialized trades		√	

Figure 25: *Example–Core Strategies Development and Strategic Action Initiatives*

The Importance of Core Strategies for Organizational Alignment

Many organizations develop an overall mission and vision, after which each department sets its own goals and objectives. While this may sound good in theory, frequently it results in silo planning leading to misalignment, impeding organizational results. See Figure 26 below.

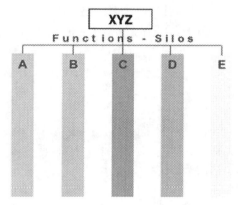

Figure 26: Silo Departmental Planning

Tip: *Core values are the cultural glue, and core strategies are functional organizational glue.*

A few years ago, my company, Raven Strategic Solutions, was asked to meet with the General Manager of a division of a Fortune 500 company. The General Manager felt strongly that he had a solid management team, excellent brands and products, and excellent resources at his disposal. Despite these assets, the division was not achieving its targets.

The division was created when the parent company acquired a prestigious brand and a similar brand at a lower price point.

Although the formation of the new division had taken place several years earlier, employees still tended to identify themselves as employees of one or the other of the two former companies. The General Manager confirmed this mentality was reinforced by the two original "teams" still using their former accounting systems.

One of the obvious challenges was misalignment between the internal departments. Although the organization was results-focused, it functioned in "silos" with each department focused only on its own results. Because of this misalignment, things fell between the cracks, causing delays and missed targets.

The "blame game" was alive and well. In addition to the internal cultural challenges, divisional staff was unclear about their priorities and overwhelmed with too many initiatives.

To transform the situation, we developed and carried out a "Breakthrough Program" that included engaging all employees in the organization, starting with the management team. Measures and targets were set to monitor progress and create a shared, future-focused vision of where they wanted the organization to be. The vision created a sense of a shared future and focus. Using the shared vision, we identified the barriers or logjams blocking the vision and the success measures targets—from this, we developed new strategies.

Among the strategies put in place were:

- Creating cross-functional, breakthrough teams to address key organizational issues
- Establishing the top 15 projects for the next fiscal year
- Improving project management skills to plan and execute projects more efficiently
- Implementing a quarterly milestone and accountability process

- Integrating the two accounting systems into one
- Implementing a series of team-building activities to help individuals connect and communicate more effectively

The division achieved its targets for the first time at the end of the fiscal year. In addition, the division won the President's award for" Best Performing Division" in their category— in all North America! Alignment horizontally and vertically toward the same shared future vision in the organization had made a critical difference. The cross-functional breakthrough teams addressed vital issues from an overall organizational perspective. Similarly, the management team established the 15 top priority projects for the year. They formed cross-functional project teams to work on the top priority projects and learned to work collaboratively rather than in silos.

Alignment starts with a set of Core Strategies, which weave together the various functions of an organization. Strategies are like a pair of snowshoes with laced rawhide webbing or a folding chair with nylon webbing both get their strength from being woven together. Core Strategies provide consistency across the organizational functions, strengthening the alignment and allowing for flexibility in how each department implements the core strategies. (See Figure 27, below, Horizontal Integration.)

"The Glue That Holds It All Together"

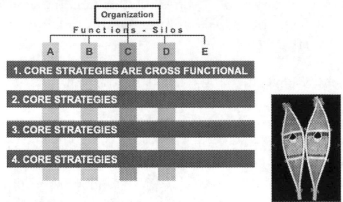

Figure 27: Horizontal Integration
Used with permission from Haines
Strategic Management Centre.

A department must be able to implement a strategy in a way appropriate to it's mission or mandate. Some clients prefer to call their strategies "organizational" rather than core. Sometimes strategies are developed that can only be carried out in one or two departments of an organization. These strategies are then called "departmental strategies" and will be included in the department's strategic plan.

Internal Alignment

Core strategies are typically developed for the organization and then cascaded to its business units or departments. Occasionally, though, the process is initiated by a business unit and then works its way upwards.

A case in point is a Health Unit that we assisted in developing a strategic plan that included seven core strategies. The following year senior leaders of the regional organization who had participated in the Health Unit planning session the previous year, went on to develop a Global Strategic Plan that included five strategic directions. When we compared the regional organization's Global Core Strategies with the Health Unit's Core Strategies, the Health Unit team was pleased to see there was a close alignment between the two plans. See Figure 28 below. This increased their confidence in the Core Strategies for the Health Unit Strategic Health Plan.

ALIGNMENT BETWEEN CHIEFS OF ONTARIO GLOBAL PLAN AND CHIEFS OF ONTARIO STRATEGIC HEALTH PLAN	
COO Global Plan Strategic Directions	COO Strategic Health Plan
Nation Building	Assert Treaty Rights for Health
Advocacy to improve a Quality of Life	Advocate and support First Nations jurisdiction to govern their own health systems
Improving relationships between FN entities	Align Ontario First Nations health system to transform the status of FN health
Managing knowledge and information	Use technology to expand access to health information
Strengthening communications	Improve the communications flow within the Ontario First Nations health system
(No Strategy)	Implement the strategic management system for sustainable change & results

Figure 28: Example–Organizational and Work Unit Alignment

Developing a Three-year Roadmap

Create a matrix indicating the year Strategic Action Initiatives will be implemented in the planning cycle. Keep in mind that you cannot accomplish everything in the first year. Attempting to do so would be overwhelming. Limiting your strategic action initiatives to approximately three per year for each strategy would result in upwards of 21 action initiatives if an organization had seven core strategies. See Figure 29: Multi-year Planning Worksheet, below.

Strategic Action Initiatives for Core Strategy #4: Safety First

	2009-2010	2010-2011	2011-2012
4.1 Implement Best Safety Practices			
a) Determine safety reporting requirements	√		
b) Establish consistent Safety Key Success Measures across the subsidiaries	√	√	
c) Train Safety Committees	√		

Figure 29: Multi-year Planning Worksheet

Deciding Which Year to Carry Out each Strategic Action Initiative

- Some actions can be carried out and completed each year.
- Some may only start in year two or three after other prerequisites have been accomplished.
- Other actions may be delayed to another year to avoid overloading a given year with too many actions.
- Some may require ongoing work across all years of the current planning cycle.

Annual Top Priorities

Once strategic action initiatives have been identified and you have determined in which year of the plan they will be carried out, the next step is to finalize the Top Priorities that must be done in the first year.

Review the priorities for the current year and decide:

- Ask yourself if the Top Priorities are manageable? And realistic?

- Decide if all the Strategic Action Initiatives listed need to be accomplished this year. Determine if any can be delayed, if so to what year?
- Once you are satisfied that Strategic Action Initiatives for the current year are necessary and manageable, decide who should have lead accountability for each one.
- Avoid the tendency to assign two or more lead persons to a specific Strategic Action Initiative - have only one person accountable for the success of a Strategic Action Initiative.
- The individual who has lead accountability for a Strategic Action Initiative is responsible for developing a workplan and decide who else should be involved in developing and implementing the plan
- Finalize the Top Priorities, ensuring that the work involved is shared among the planning team or management team members.

Summarize the current year's Top Priority Strategic Action Initiatives in a one- or two-page Top Annual Priority Worksheet that lists the Strategic Action Initiatives for each Core Strategy, the name of the individual employee who will have responsibility for it.

The Top Priorities Worksheet is a valuable reference tool in your management meetings to review and update the Strategic Action Initiatives during the year. See an example of an annual top priority action plan in Figure 30, see below.

20XX-20XY Annual Top Priority Actions

*These are the key "Must Do" actions -- focus, focus, focus -- in addition to
(1) the day-to-day operations, and (2) any other tasks you can complete.*

Organizational Strategies	Lead Accountability	2010-2011 Top Priorities
1. Strengthen Relationships with Key Stakeholders	Tony	1.1. Implement organizational communications strategy with a focus on different stakeholder groups
	Lillian	1.2. Continue relationship building with key stakeholder groups
	Ann	1.4. Measure Stakeholder Satisfaction with the organization and our services
2. Increase Revenue Streams	Tony	2.3 Invest in a major business opportunity
	Ann	2.5. Access ABC Initiatives Fund
	Doug	2.6. Work with the XYZ Board to seek new sources of funding

Figure 30: Top Annual Priorities

Note of caution:

- Many organizations tend to take on too many Strategic Action Initiatives each year, which results in overwhelm, discouragement if they are unable to accomplish them.
- Another trap is an imbalance of workload, with some individuals having too many top priorities and others having too few or none.
- The key is to complete the process with an achievable set of top priority actions doable in the current year.

Determine the "Wildly Important" Initiatives

Many years ago, I had encouraged clients to choose multiple initiatives, but now realize that doing so can diffuse efforts by splitting employee's focus and energies in too many directions. The more we try to do, the less we end up accomplishing!

Conventional Thinking	4 DX Principle
All of our initiatives are Priority # 1. We can successfully multitask and succeed at five, seven, or ten. All we need to do is work harder and longer.	Many of our initiative are important but only one or two are wildly important, calling them WIG's for short. They are the objectives we must achieve. Our finest effort can only be given to one or two wildly important ones at a time.

Figure 31: Identify WIG (Widely Important Goals)
Source: Adapted from The 4 Dimensions of Execution

While it is difficult to say no to other good ideas and goals, by focusing on a few clear and realistic initiatives considered "wildly important," companies can achieve greater success in the areas that matter. One example of a company that has done this is Apple, whose CEO admits to saying no to good ideas every day. Yet, they are a $40 billion dollar company with a limited number of successful products.

They set their own "Wildly important" action initiatives that align with their vision and realize their Key Success Measures. By doing so, they become more committed to the process and take more ownership over the achievement of these initiatives. The authors of 4D say that a good WIG must be both worthy and winnable.

The global telecom organization restructuring and realignment project, mentioned earlier, developed a strategic plan with seven core strategies to meet the changing needs of its internal clients. They strategically chose to only implement one core strategy initially, that was worthy and winnable, resulting in being six months of ahead of executing their strategic plan, and achieving high level of approval, 95% satisfaction rating from stakeholders.

In a study conducted by McKinsey, when top executives compared their highest priorities, only 2 out of 23 priorities appeared on all the top executives' lists. Although all 23 priorities are important, only a few "wildly important" goals are likely to make a significant difference in helping the organization achieve its most important objectives. We must identify those actions that will have the greatest impact in helping us achieve those "wildly important" goals.

Research has shown that only 20% of all activities performed generate 80% of an organization's results. The activities we focus on must make all the difference in achieving our success.

In Summary.... the two most vital areas of the planning process are to:

1. Develop your scorecard or dashboard with key performance indicators and targets to measure progress towards the organization's desired future, your mission, vision, and values.
2. Secondly, develop a powerful set of Core Strategies to be implemented across the organization to achieve your targets/ goals. For each strategy, determine the strategic action initiatives to be carried out, and the year each will be done in the current planning cycle.

You can either take action or you can hang back and hope for a miracle. Miracles are great, but they are so unpredictable.

Peter Drucker (1909-2005)

LEVEL 3 -
DEPARTMENATAL
PLANNING

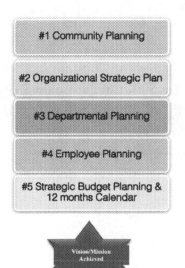

#1 Community Planning — Engage members in setting direction

#2 Organizational Strategic Plan — Create organizational strategic plan

#3 Departmental Planning — Align departments with organizational plan and create multi year plans

#4 Employee Planning — Set objectives to implement department priorities and key job description responsibilities and work plans

#5 Strategic Budget Planning & 12 months Calendar — Develop strategic budget to implement priorities and an annual calendar

Vision/Mission Achieved

The next chapter explains the importance of cascading the Organizational Plan to Departments to create a multi-year Departmental strategic and operational plan reflecting community member priorities.

Chapter 9: Step 6:
Departmental Planning

Cascading the plan for alignment

One goal of strategic planning is to develop an organizational plan and "cascade" it to each department to create departmental plans that align with the organizational plan. Otherwise, departments and employees are going in different directions, resulting in diffused energy and decreased momentum, negatively impacting organizational results.

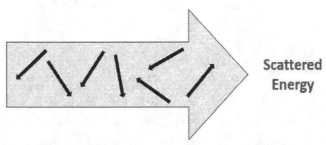

Figure 32: Misaligned Organization

Some organizations develop an overall strategic plan, but its departments create their plans without considering the organizational strategies, resulting in cross-functional misalignment. Such siloed planning can negatively impact your mission and results. Failure to align departmental plans with the organizational plan puts the organization's strategic plan at risk. Bottlenecks can occur, as well as errors and lost opportunities.

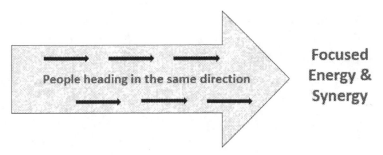

Figure 33: Aligned Organization

The key to alignment is to implement a set of core strategies to increase consistent approaches across its departments and work units, allowing for flexibility in their implementation. Better alignment leads to better results.

A McKinsey study reported smaller companies, using a more collaborative approach to strategy development tended to achieve somewhat better results than those that used a corporate-led approach.

The larger the organization, the more likely a corporate-led strategy is used. Such strategies are formulated based on targets set at the corporate level in areas such as growth, profit, or market share. Corporate-directed strategies are handed to the business unit leaders to implement at the operational level. Almost a quarter of business units then develop their strategic plan based on the corporate targets without the opportunity to provide significant input. Their plans are then reviewed and approved at the corporate level.

Although executives at the corporate level may perceive their process as collaborative, managers involved in strategy formulation at the business unit level more often view strategy development as corporate-directed.

Leaders of smaller organizations more frequently report taking a collaborative approach to planning in which departments are involved in the organizational planning.

> *Executives are most pleased with their*
> *business units if they work at companies*
> *that apply many best practices to the*
> *process and foster collaboration between*
> *corporate and business unit managers.*
> The McKinsey Quarterly

Cascading the Plan

The goal of cascading the plan is to ensure consistency across the organization horizontally and vertically while allowing flexibility in how a business unit or department implements it.

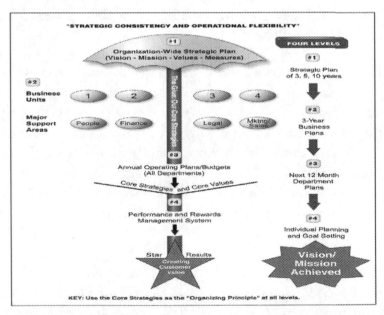

Figure 34: Cascade the Plan
Used with permission of Haines Centre
for Strategic Management

According to a McKinsey Global Survey, most executives agree that their organization's approaches to formulating business unit strategy help to align business leaders with the corporate strategy, guaranteeing a commitment to its implementation and ensuring that those who execute the strategy are involved in developing it. But only a minority agrees that their approach fosters creativity, incorporates priorities of employees at different levels, and effectively identifies growth opportunities outside of the core business.

The Results Certainty Strategic Management Systems allow for consistency and flexibility as a department follows the same five steps.

1—Environmental Scanning—'Begin with the end in mind.' Building on the organizational trends, ask if the future trends are likely to impact the department and its key functions and likely potential implications. Clients have found it helpful to use the future organizational trends, their potential implications as a springboard for identifying departmental trends that are likely to impact the department and its key functions.

2—Desired Future State—Develop or revisit the departmental mission to ensure alignment with the organizational mission and update it as needed—an organization needs only one vision. Check alignment with the organizational vision and mission by discussing what the department contributes to it. Similarly, engage employees to consider their contribution to the organization's vision and mission of the department.

3—Feedback Measures—Although key success measures and key performance indicators are established at the organizational level, they are monitored by the department responsible for them. In addition to the organizational key success measures, each department also develops operational key performance indicators and targets to measure progress towards their departmental and business unit's mission.

4—Current State Assessment—Similar to the current state assessment process used to develop the organizational strategic plan, each department assesses the obstacles and gaps between where it wants to be and where it is currently. Our clients have found it useful and time-saving to build on the organization's current state assessment. The process of identifying the department's SWOT analysis and actions provides valuable input to developing the department's multi-year plan.

Core Strategies and Multi-Year Operational Plan

The second part of the Current State Assessment phase is to develop the department's operational plan to implement the organization's Core Strategies. Each department considers the organization's strategies and if they can implement them in a way that is appropriate to its mission or mandate. The unit develops its strategic action initiatives to close the gaps between where it wants to be from and actions to realize its mission.

In developing its departmental Strategic Action Initiatives, each department assesses the obstacles and gaps between where it wants to be from where it is currently. Based on the desired change, the department identifies 5 to 10 Strategic Action Initiatives to implement over the plan's lifespan.

After identifying the essential Strategic Action Initiatives for the department to implement over the planning period, the departmental team decides the year they will carry out each over the next three years. A final step in developing your departmental plan is to review the list of top priorities for the current year and decide who will have lead accountability for each.

Persons responsible for the Top Annual Priorities will then develop work plans assigned to them. Chapter 9, Developing Work Plans, provides ideas and best practices for developing work plans to produce desired results and changes.

5—Implementation of the Plan—Once you have developed your departmental strategic and a multi-year operational plan, your top annual priorities are established, and work plans created, it is time to prepare to implement your plan. Chapter 10, Implementing Your Plan, provides ideas and best practices for shifting from planning to action.

Integrated Organizational and Departmental Planning

When one of my clients evaluated their strategic planning process, one of the senior managers commented that it seemed redundant to go through the organizational planning process again with his department. His statement presented a challenge and an opportunity for considering other options for departmental planning. After analyzing various options, we agreed to develop and implement an integrated organizational and departmental planning process.

The Integrated Organizational and Departmental Planning Process

The process started with each department reviewing their progress, achievements, and challenges over the past year, from which they identified what they had learned. In the whole organization planning process, each department presented to the other departmental teams highlights from their department's review from which we identified the overall organizational achievements, challenges, and learning.

The whole organizational team then updated the Environmental Trends, the implications of the trends, and the trends that were most likely to occur, and those that would have the most significant impact if they did. The divisional teams then developed and updated the trends likely to impact their division.

Similarly, we briefly reviewed, the organizational mission, vision, and the core values. Divisions then reviewed and updated their desired future vision and mission, and individual employees reflected on their contribution to the organizational mission and vision and to the departmental mission. In preparation for updating the organizational Key Success Measures and progress towards their annual and 3-year targets, divisions reviewed their progress. They re-established their 3-year targets for reporting to the whole organization.

In developing or updating the Current State Assessment, we developed a Current State Assessment at the organizational level and used it to update the Core Strategies and Strategic Action Initiatives. Using the Current State Assessment and Core Strategies, Strategic Action Initiatives, and Annual Top Priorities, each division then updated its Strategic Action Initiatives and which employee would be responsible for each. Using its Divisional Annual Top Priorities, divisional employees developed work plans, a topic which we will cover in the next chapter.

Employee Involvement in the Planning Process

According to the Aberdeen research on developing a high-performance culture, the number one activity of top-performing organizations reported that the single most significant impact on employee performance is aligning individual employee goals with overall organizational goals. When supervisors and employees have agreed on goals, it has a tremendous effect on performance results.

Although it may not be possible for all employees to be involved in the organizational strategy planning [Level 2 – Figures 35A &B], it is crucial for them to be involved in the departmental/ business unit planning. Such involvement deepens understanding of both the organizational and departmental plan and their role in it.

As recommend earlier, whenever possible, the community and employees should be engaged in the process.

5 Level Integrated Planning Model

#1 Community Vision & Goals	Engage members in envisioning the desired future and priorities
#2 Org. Strategic Plan for 3-5 years	Operationalize the Community vision and priorities
#3 Dept. Plans 2-3 years	Align departments with organizational plan and create multi-year dept. plans
#4 Employee Objective Setting and Work Planning	Set objectives to implement departmental priorities and key job description responsibilities
#5 Annual Plans and Budgets for next 12 months	Develop annual plans to implement departmental 3-4 years priorities

Vision/Mission Achieved

Figure 35 A: 5 Level Planning

When it is not possible to engage the community, the planning model is reduced to 4 level.

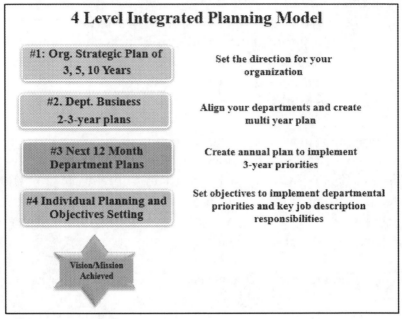

Figure 35 B: 4 Level Planning

Summary

It is essential to cascade planning to the department or business unit level. This is where the "rubber hits the road," where strategy is turned into action to bring about results, and anticipated changes are realized.

> *Cooperation gets teams pulling together. Staying focused on the organization's mission ensures they pull together in the right direction.*
>
> Eric Harvey

LEVEL 4 - EMPLOYEE PLANNING

#1 Community Planning — Engage members in setting direction

#2 Organizational Strategic Plan — Create organizational strategic plan

#3 Departmental Planning — Align departments with organizational plan and create multi year plans

#4 Employee Planning — Set objectives to implement department priorities and key job description responsibilities and work plans

#5 Strategic Budget Planning & 12 months Calendar — Develop strategic budget to implement priorities and an annual calendar

Vision/Mission Achieved

The next chapter provides a process for Employee Planning, involving them in the planning process to set objectives and develop work plans to implement their delegated departmental strategic action initiatives and other key job specific priorities for the coming year

Chapter 10: Employee Planning

Setting objectives & developing work plans

Vision without action is 'wish dreaming';
vision with action can change the world.

Joel Barker

First Set Employee Objectives

Early in my strategic planning career, I believed that if a group had a clear vision for the future, it would just happen— that employees would automatically do whatever was needed to realize it. I have learned that if you are serious about realizing your desired future and your goals, it is essential to develop work plans to achieve them.

Executing strategies requires clarity about how to turn them into results. Contrary to what people often say, you don't implement a strategic plan; nor do you implement a three-year or one-year plan; you implement your top priority strategic action initiatives, all of which require work or action plans. A work or action plan spells out what, how, when, who, and the resources needed to implement each Strategic Action Initiative for each Core Strategy.

Success is planned-in-advance. Nowhere is this truer than when it comes to developing work plans for success. Unless work plans are well thought through, they jeopardize the mission, vision, key success measures, and the strategies will not get implemented.

Developing Work Plans

Developing employees work plans pays big dividends. Research indicates every one hour of planning saves four hours in execution. Why would this be so? If you are building a structure, delays happen when the proper materials are not in place and ordered last minute. Ineffective planning and scheduling may result in attempting to build in the wrong season of the year; construction workers may not be available when needed. Some organizations resist investing the time and energy required to develop work or action plans. Planning is often considered a waste of time when desired results aren't achieved.

Well-developed work plans give the developer clear direction for what is to be done and when. Failure happens when the person has not carefully planned what to do or approaches carrying out the Strategic Action Initiative haphazardly. Typically, essential steps are forgotten, causing mistakes, bad outcomes, or delays, causing stress and feeling overloaded by a flurry of last-minute activities.

Well-developed work plans with costs feed into strategic budgeting for resources so you can estimate the time and costs needed to implement its strategic priorities. Action or work plans are major or mini-project plans. If a Strategic Action Initiative is a priority, it deserves a work or project plan for successful implementation.

What Goes Into the Work or Project Plan?

What—the Major Actions needed to implement Strategic Action Initiatives.

How—the Specific Tasks to carry out each Major Action and the criteria for How to Measure it meets quality standards.

When—an estimate of the Time to carry out the tasks involved in each Major Action as well as the estimated completion and start dates

Who—the Persons whose assistance or expertise is needed to accomplish the Major Actions and Specific Tasks. Who Else might be involved?

Resources—the Persons, Materials, and Supplies needed to accomplish the Major Actions and Specific Tasks and estimated Cost.

_____ Core Strategy: _____

_____ Strategic Action Intiative: _____

Major Action Steps List the major action steps to achieve the objective.	Specific Tasks List the specific tasks to carry out each major action step	How to Measure?	By When?	Who Else to Involve?	Support/ Resources
			Est. Time		Cost $$

Figure 36: Work Plan (Core Elements)

Developing Employee Work Plans

Experience has shown that developing effective and complete work plans typically takes three steps:

STEP ONE—Drafting Work Plans

In step one, the developer creates a first draft, listing the Major Actions needed to implement the Strategic Action Initiative. One way to make it easier and faster to develop work plans is developing a Mind Map with the name of the Strategic Action

Initiative in the middle of the page, with branches added for each of the Major Actions. Use a one- or two-word title for each Major Action.

Mind maps are helpful to jump-start the flow of ideas by inviting one or two colleagues to join you in a mind mapping session.

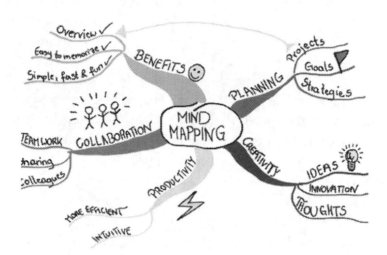

Figure 37: Example—Mind Map

Major Actions

Ask yourself the following questions:

1. What are the Preparatory actions needed to realize this Strategic Action Initiative? (E.g., ordering supplies, contracting with others, preparing submissions, meeting with the project team, and so on)
2. What are the significant Implementation actions? (E.g., carrying out the task, delivering the program)
3. What are the significant Completion actions? (E.g., evaluating outcomes with your internal or external client as well as with other members of the project team)

Check that you have included all three types of actions in your mind map and your work plan.

Specific Tasks

The extent to which a work plan includes the tasks needed to implement each Major Action determines the work plan's effectiveness. If you are familiar with the mind mapping process, adding specific tasks is like drawing small branches from the primary branches.

Ideally, you want to identify three to five tasks for each Major Action. If you have more than five is an indication that you are working with more than one Major Action and need to split them into well-defined Major Action initiatives. If you have only one or two tasks, the tasks are likely part of a larger action, or you have not thought through how to carry out each Major Action. Any time you get stuck in coming up with ideas, take a break and return to it. Or bounce your ideas off a colleague or ask others for ideas.

Often, when you explain to someone what is needed to complete a Major Action, you expand your thinking about the tasks involved, you get unstuck. Include these ideas and anything else that comes to mind. You can make refinements later.

For each Major Action and its specific tasks, ask yourself, "How long would it take to do each task? One CEO with whom I worked tells employees in his organization to add a third of the estimated time, as most things take longer than what they initially calculated.

If you have developed similar work or projects plans in the past, you can consult them as historical records to better estimate the Time needed. If you find yourself working on a similar project in the future, you will appreciate quickly referring to the Time estimates for these tasks. For myself, I do not mind being wrong once, even twice, but after the third experience, I want to learn from my mistakes! Nowhere is this truer than in estimating Time.

Some projects will have an assigned or previously scheduled completion date, such as fiscal year-end or an annual general meeting. Most deadlines or completion dates are discretionary, allowing you to decide the date they need for completion.

Based on your completion date and the amount of work involved, decide the start date for various Major Actions. One tendency is starting all projects or Strategic Action Initiative work plans simultaneously. Most people think they can accomplish a great deal in the first quarter of their work plans and list more Strategic Action Initiatives than what is possible to complete. Re-assess priorities regarding what to do first and what you delay. Getting the timing right is one of the biggest challenges in developing and implementing realistic work plans. Most of us are overly ambitious on paper, causing burnout. Be prepared to adjust your timing and scheduling based on your experience from previous quarters.

A final step is estimating the Cumulative Time and Costs at the bottom of each work plan. For each Major Action and its specific tasks, ask yourself, "How long would it take to do each task?"

People

Another consideration is the availability of the people who will be critical contributors to the Major Actions or Specific Tasks. Determine whose expertise and assistance are needed. Get their input into the Major Actions and Specific Tasks, discuss timing, and check their availability. Based on their feedback, you may need to revise the actions, tasks, or timing based on their feedback.

Resources and Costs

Consider the resources needed for implementing your work plans and anything that will require a financial investment or budgetary approval.

Resources typically include professional services that you would hire or contract and additional supplies, materials, and equipment that would need to procure.

Ask yourself what additional resources and external and professional services are needed. List the supplementary materials, supplies, or equipment required. Include these in the total Financial investment (Time and costs) at the bottom of each work plan.

Test Your Work Plan for Completeness

Imagine that you have won a trip worldwide; taking a leave of absence depends on preparing another employee to take over your Strategic Action Initiatives and its work plans. Your work plan must be sufficiently detailed so that someone can successfully carry out the work plan.

STEP TWO—Group Review of Work Plans

Earlier I mentioned that developing work plans usually is a three-step process. In step two, we recommend a group review of the work plans of each department. There are two benefits to holding a review of work plans. One is that it forces employees to complete their work plans—it gets them done.

Secondly, employees receive feedback and valuable input to strengthen the completeness of their work plans.

STEP THREE—Fine-Tuning Employee Work Plans

In this step, employees make needed changes to their work plans using the team's feedback.

Who Should Be Involved in Developing Work Plans?

Many years ago, when I was facilitating a strategic planning process for a First Nation, we had a high level of citizen involvement in various phases of the planning process, including creating a mission, vision, and core values for the First Nation, assessing the current situation, and determining essential strategies. While their involvement helped increase community commitment to the plan, they could not contribute meaningfully to the development of work plans outside of their area of knowledge. The lesson is to engage people, they must have the knowledge and experience to contribute meaningfully to developing work plans.

Furthermore, work plans should be developed by those responsible for implementing them, typically employees, with input from other stakeholders. Usually, these are persons who have functional responsibility for the Strategic Action Initiatives and the knowledge and skills to carry them out.

Marcelene Anderson

Summary

To accomplish great things, we
must dream as well as act.

Anatole France

Whatever you can do, or dream you can, begin it.
Boldness has genius, power, and magic in it.

Johann Goethe

LEVEL 5 – STRATEGIC BUDGETING

#1 Community Planning	Engage members in setting direction
#2 Organizational Strategic Plan	Create organizational strategic plan
#3 Departmental Planning	Align departments with organizational plan and create multi year plans
#4 Employee Planning	Set objectives to implement department priorities and key job description responsibilities and work plans
#5 Strategic Budget Planning & 12 months Calendar	Develop strategic budget to implement priorities and an annual calendar

Vision/Mission Achieved

The next chapter provides an overview about developing a strategic budget for the investment to implement the strategic priorities of the organization as well as to develop a strategic management annual calendar.

Chapter 11: Strategic Budgeting

Determining the investment

The only good strategic plan gets implemented

Marcelene Anderson

If you have ever built a house or remodeled one, you know the importance of establishing a budget before beginning the project.

Similarly, aligning your strategic plan and budget is crucial to realizing your plan. Without the necessary resources, you cannot implement your plan.

Before implementing your strategic plan, the management of your organization reviews the completed departmental work plans and the costs estimate of the plans to develop an annual strategic budget to realize the annual plan.

The annual budgeting and resource allocation is done after developing your strategic plan. Aligning your strategic plan and budget is crucial to realizing your plan. Without the necessary resources, you cannot implement your plan.

As mentioned in Chapter 1, scheduling ample time for strategic budgeting is vital not to rush the process. After completing their work plans, I have seen organizations realize that the cumulative costs of the strategic action initiatives exceed their anticipated resources. Establishing a strategic budget to achieve/support your top priorities is a challenge.

A budget is strategic when the allocation of funds is determined by the annual priorities crucial to achieving the organization's vision. According to Haines, to be strategic, budgeting and resource allocation must the following five criteria:

1. Reinforces and focuses on your Desired Future and Key Success Measures/Goals.
2. Supports your strategic plan's top annual priorities under each core strategy.
3. The criteria for your budgeting decisions must be the top priorities from your strategic plan.
4. Your budget priorities match up closely with the core strategies.
5. Results in your being able to fund and carry out day-to-day business as well as be able to support needed future changes.

Developing Your Strategic Budget

1. Working at the department level, each department has established and reviewed the cost of its annual work plans.
2. Create a matrix with the names of your department's strategic action initiatives by employee or role, along with its estimated cost, into a Core Strategies (SAI) matrix. See Figure 38 below and total the cost of the SAIs by column.

Department XYZ Annual Strategic Budget						
Core Strategies	All Employees					
	Emp. 1	Emp. 2	Emp. 3	Emp. 4	Emp. 5	Total
	#SAIs $	#SAIs $	#SAIs $	#SAIs $	#SAIs $	#SAIs $
1:						
2.						
3:						
4:						
5:						
Total	#SAIs $$	#SAIs $$	#SAIs $$	#SAIs $$	#SAIs $$	#SAIs $$

Figure 38: Department Annual Strategic Budget

Using your matrix above, list the number of SAIs assigned to each employee/role.

Checklist – The SAI supports the:

- Your Desired Future, e.g., Mission and Vision
- Key Success Measures/Goals
- Each SAI is a Top Priority
- There is a balance of SAI effort required within the team

3. Forward all Departmental Annual Strategic Budgets to your organization's strategic plan coordinator to compile or create a matrix for the group meeting so that each department can report its SAIs by Core Strategy and the estimated total cost by Core Strategy.

Annual Strategic Budget						
Core Strategies	All Departments					
	Dept. A	Dept. B	Dept. C	Dept. D	Dept. E	Total
	# SAIs $$	# SAIs $$	# SAIs $$	# SAIs $$	# SAIs $$	# SAIs $$
1:						
2:						
3:						
4:						
5:						
Total	#SAIs $$	#SAIs $$	#SAIs $$	#SAIs $$	#SAIs $$	#SAIs $$

Figure 39: Annual Strategic Budget

Next, determine and list the level of priority among the Top Priorities, e.g., High, Medium, or Lower Priority. To decide, consider the impact or contribution of each strategic action initiative to the mission and vision as well to achieving the Key Performance Indicators or goals. See Figure 40 SAIs by Top Priorities above & below the matrix

SAIs by Top Priorities					
Strategic Action Initiative	Priority Level:			Cost	Dept
	HP	MP	LP		

Figure 40: SAIs By Top Priorities

You now have the Total Cost of implementing all Top Priorities for all departments. In addition, you have several priorities for each department, and ensure each department has at least one or two High Priorities.

4. Creating a workable budget is where the challenge begins. Maybe you are lucky and have more funds available or anticipated for the next budget cycle from various sources. List and total all revenue sources of funds. Indicate if funds are Allocated √ or are Unallocated √.

5. At this point, you are undoubtedly trying various budget combinations to fund High Priorities, Medium Priorities, as well as many Lower Priorities as possible. Additionally, ensure that you include priorities for each department.

You may be faced with finding new and innovative ways to increase revenue and income and reduce costs to address budgeting challenges. Encourage new initiatives and find options.

Your strategic budget must be integrated with and linked to your strategic plan, work plans, and annual plans. Integrating the strategic budgeting cycle in the organization can take up to 1 or 2 years with 40% - 70% incremental implementation in the first year.

Haines says the key is not to cut or increase budgets evenly across the board but to make simultaneous budget cuts and additions based on your strategic criteria. He continues, rather than a fixed budget driving your strategic plan, the plan should drive your budget.

Develop a Comprehensive Yearly Strategic Yearly Calendar

One more step before implementing your plan is developing a Strategic Map for the year ahead. The purpose of the Strategic Map is to lay out the key activities essential to ensuring consistent and excellent implementation of your strategic management system in the year ahead. Figure 41 depicts an example of a Strategic Management Yearly Calendar below.

To implement and keep our strategic plan, these are the actions we will put into place.

Date	Meetings
March 202X	Finalize the Strategic Plan and Strategic Budget
	Prepare for Implementation
April 202X	Launch the Plan
	All Staff Communication Meeting
	Monthly Strategic Management Team (SMT) Meeting
May 202X	Monthly SMT Meeting
June 202x	Monthly SMT Meeting
July 202x	Monthly SMT Meeting
	Hold Quarter #2 Progress Meeting
	All Staff Communication Meeting
August 202X	Monthly SMT Meeting
September 202X	Monthly SMT Meeting
October 202x	Monthly SMT Meeting
	Hold Quarter #2 Progress Meeting
	All Staff Communication Meeting

November 202X	Review & Update the Strategic Plan for Year 2, Sessions 1 & 2
	Monthly SMT Meeting
December 202X	Review & Update the Strategic Plan for Year 2, Sessions 3
	Begin Departmental Planning
	Monthly SMT Meeting
January 202X	Hold Quarter #3 Progress Meeting & All Staff Meeting
	Chief & Council Feedback & Integration to Strategic Plan
	Citizen Feedback Sessions & Integration
	Begin Departmental Planning
February 202X	Complete Departmental Planning
	Monthly SMT Meeting
March 203X	Finalize the Strategic Plan and Strategic Budget
	Prepare for Year 2 Implementation
April 202X	Quarter 4 Progress Review
	Implementation Launch of Year 2 Plan & All Staff Meeting
	Monthly SMT Meeting

Figure 41: Example: Strategic Management Yearly Calendar

Section 2:

Implementing Your Strategic Plan

Chapter 12: Step 6: Implementing Your Strategic Plan

Turning plans into results

The only good strategic plan is one that gets implemented.

Marcelene Anderson

Do not skip or skim this chapter – it is the most important chapter in the book. To discover why consider the historical story below:

Imagine the year is 1969, July 16th when the US launched its spaceship to put a man on the moon. Some of you eagerly gathered around a TV to watch this momentous occasion. Others of you have seen dozens if not hundreds of images of this event.

Millions of dollars and tens of millions man person hours had been invested in the project. The actual cost was $25.4 billion (1973) $153 billion (2018).

What if after spending millions of dollars and person hours on the Apollo project, Nassau delayed and ignored the launching the project? It would have been unthinkable! Imagine the disappointment. An outcry that the US was losing its competitive standing in the world stage! What does this have to do with implementing a strategic plan?

Let's explore that idea with the Apollo One Project:

- It was based on a significant, bold vision.
- The project had the support and was a top priority of senior management, none less than the President of the United States of America.
- A huge investment was made in the planning and preparations.
- It had a definite launch date.
- All key players, the astronauts, mission control staff and others had received countless hours of training.
- Resources–financial, materials and people were available to support the project and its launch.
- Communications that the lead up to the launch event, the actual launch event, ongoing progress, all of which was communicated using the media available at the time.
- Ongoing communication between the space crew and mission control, frequent check-ins.
- Problems and issues were dealt with as a part of the mission.
- The completion of the mission, re-entry, was carefully planned.
- The team debriefed their experience, its accomplishments, challenges, and what they learned and would do differently another time.

What can we learn from the Apollo project - the same thinking and practices are essential for planning for self-determination or other plans?

Each of the previous 5 steps is important to develop a powerful plan. This is chapter, Step 6, on implementation is the most vital – unless a plan is implemented it has no value. It would be a like a failure to launch the Apollo One.

Having a good strategy and strategic plan is essential to achieving results. But it is *not* enough.

Results are determined by how well you execute your plans.

> *An execution with a B strategy is better than an*
> *A strategy with a B execution.*

Ram Charan

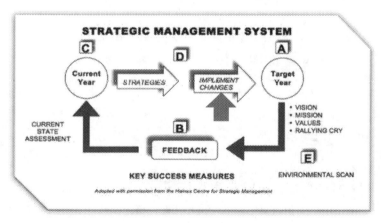

Figure 42: Strategic Management System – Implement Changes

Between planning and executing, of the two, executing plans is more challenging. Organizations do not fail in planning but typically fail in implementation.

The authors of "The 4 Disciplines of Execution" believe that while strategy sets the direction, it is how you *execute* that strategy that drives an organization to achieve sustained superior results.

90% of plans fail to deliver expected results. Shocking!

According to Haines, pioneer of the Systems Thinking Approach to Strategic Management®, developing a strategic and operational plan will get you only 20% of the way to the results that you want and your desired future. Successfully *implementing* your plans moves you another 40% of the way.

Despite the importance of successfully implementing strategic and operational plans the Economist Intelligence Unit estimates that organizations realize just 60% of the potential value of their strategies.

This is due in part to not systematically implementing plans, including not systematically monitoring progress and keeping plans on track.

The Harvard Business Review estimates the ROI from traditional planning approaches to be 34% or less.

Barriers to Implementation

Assuming that the organizational strategic plan was cascaded to the business units or its departments to create operational plans aligned with it and employees have objectives and work plans, aligned with their departmental and the organizational strategic plan, many things get in the way of implementing plans including but not limited to:

- Absence of management support
- Distractions—getting off track

- Changing priorities
- Ineffective day-to-day self-management
- Weak accountability systems
- Communication breakdowns
- Misalignment between departments
- Difficulty monitoring results—do not have systems
- The corporate culture does not support achieving results
- Low level of management to leadership and employee capacity
- Lack of implementation know-how
- Insufficient resources to implement the strategy
- Implementation is left to chance

Keeping the Plan on Track

In the airline industry, once a flight has taken off for its destination, it easily drifts off course due to wind and other conditions. The pilot must continually monitor progress to bring the plane back on to its intended flight path. This process is called "craving."

Similarly, once an organization begins the implementation of its plan, it can go off course too, requiring a process to monitor progress and bring performance and results back on track. Unfortunately, according to one McKinsey article, only 19% of companies say that they review corporate strategy on an ongoing basis.

> *However beautiful the strategy, you should*
> *occasionally look at the results.*

Sir Winston Churchill 1874-1965

The two-fold objectives of the Implementation phase are to:

- Successfully implement the plan and systematically monitor progress towards planned results as well as to make continuous improvements.
- Build and sustain a high-performance organization, which has the capacity to achieve results over the long term and day-to- day.

Implementation Best Practices

To succeed in executing its plan an organization needs a defined implementation system. Over the past decade of assisting organizations to successfully implement plans as well as learning from those which have not, we have identified 10 Best Implementation Practices:

1. Secure Senior Management Support
2. Put in Place an Implementation System
3. Hold Implementation Launch sessions
4. Enhance Management and Employee Capacity
5. Strengthen Individual Employee Self Leadership
6. Hold Weekly One-on-One Supervisor and Employee Meetings
7. Hold Monthly Management Team Meetings and Departmental Team Meetings
8. Hold Quarterly Review Meetings
9. Ongoing Communication & Reporting
10. Review and Update the Strategic Plan Annually

1. Secure Senior Management Support

Senior executives recognize the importance of strategy implementation, but a majority admit that their companies fall short, according to *Why good strategies fail: lessons for the*

C-suite, an Economist Intelligence Unit report, sponsored by the Project Management Institute (PMI).

Some eighty-eight percent of senior executives reported that executing strategic initiatives successfully will be "essential" or "very important" for their organizations' competitiveness over the next three years. Yet 61% of them acknowledged that their firms often struggle to bridge the gap between strategy formulation and its day-to-day implementation.

Senior management has a vital role in the success of strategy formulation and implementation for their organizations and can support each by:

- Committing to a planning process for the organization, scheduling sufficient time, providing the necessary resources, and committing to a system to implement the strategic plan once it is developed/updated.
- Participating in planning sessions, conveying its importance, and not just leaving it for lower-level staff; kicking off the sessions by setting context and expectations, sharing ideas, encouraging others to share ideas, providing closing remarks for what was gained, etc.
- Taking a lead role in launching the implementation process. Like the planning process, providing context, conveying expectations, actively participating, encouraging others, and providing closing remarks.
- Always (as often as possible) referring to the organization's purpose, mission, and vision in meetings and conversations. Make them come alive and inspire others! Paint word pictures.
- Being visible and participating throughout the implementation process.

- Making short progress reports, having virtual round tables in which employees can ask questions.
- Recognizing the contributions of others.
- Encouraging the team and team members.
- Maintaining the implementation schedule, e.g., treating one-on-one meetings 'sacred' to convey to others that they are important. Keep in mind managers and supervisors will do the same with their employees.
- Wrapping-up the fiscal year or planning year with a special address about accomplishments, recognizing challenges and gratitude, as well as hopes for the next year in the planning cycle.

2. Put in Place an Implementation System

On a few occasions, I have encountered leaders who have had said, 'We can take it from here.' Sadly, they are saying, we are sufficiently satisfied with the status quo that we do not want to do anything different.

Without a defined implementation system and senior management commitment to implementation, it rarely happens. For those organizations that want to achieve a different future and results, putting in place an implementation system is the means to make it happen.

The key components of an implementation schedule include:

- Establishing an implementation schedule including all major types of events/activities by month
- Launching the plan with multiple audiences:
  - o The board of directors/Council
  - o The management team
  - o All employees

- o   Stakeholders, e.g., citizens
- Educating managers and employees on implementation
- Training managers to hold 15-20 minutes weekly or biweekly person to person or virtual Check-In meetings with each of their employees
- Training employees on self-leadership to accomplish results
- Installing reporting software and training or a progress tracking system
- Holding weekly management meetings
- Having monthly departmental team meetings
- Holding quarterly milestone management meetings
- All staff communication meetings to acknowledge progress, what's next, how the organization is dealing with challenges
- Regular communications, via progress, success stories on social media, bulletin boards, newsletters, etc.
- End of year review of progress towards the strategic plan and lessons learned

Benefits of an implementation system

- Maintain focus
- Real time accountability
- Maintain alignment across the organization and departments
- Continuous progress and recalibration of plans

The Raven Implementation Certainty System™ helps organizations to integrate the foregoing elements into a system to consistently achieve results, while avoiding implementation breakdown, failure, and disappointment.

3. Hold Implementation Launches

It is vital for an organization to hold an Implementation Launch session with the senior management team, another with its employees, and a third one with its citizens/membership to create momentum towards the implementation of your strategic plan for results.

In my experience, many good plans have been abandoned before implementation has occurred, resulting in "SPOTS", Strategic Plan on Top Shelf. Some leaders develop plans and then go back to business as usual. Why develop a plan designed to bring about change if you do not want to change?

By its very nature, strategic planning involves reassessing where you want to be in the future, specifying the targets and results you want to achieve, then developing the strategies and actions needed to bring about the desired changes.

Failure to deliberately implement your plan results in more of the same old action or behavior and loss of potential momentum.

> *A plan will not implement itself. It requires a deliberate launch and a systematic process to implement it.*

Marcelene Anderson

Just as sports events have an official start, such as when the puck is dropped at a hockey game, or the first ball is pitched at a baseball game, or when the conductor drops his baton to start a concert, an organization needs a formal event to signal that it is now in motion and the implementation has begun.

An implementation launch may vary: the management team may hold a special launch event, sharing their plans with each other and declaring what they intend to achieve in the coming year. They might hold an all- staff event announcing that the new implementation year has begun, reviewing highlights of the plan, and declaring what the organization intends to accomplish. Such an event can be a celebration of the year ahead, like a New Year's celebration. Head offices can hold a "web launch" for departments that are scattered regionally. There is always a way to declare and symbolize that you have begun to implement your plan.

Similarly, a department may hold a launch event to review its plan for the coming years and what it intends to achieve in the year ahead. In addition, a launch event may be held with its citizens to inform them on the updated 3-year plan and plan for the next fiscal year.

Whatever approach is taken, the launch event is an opportunity to reinforce the organization's mission/purpose and vision, what is unique about this year's plans, and employees' roles in realizing the Key Success Areas, Performance Indicator's to monitor progress towards its vision and key performance indicators (KPIs) as well as introduce the core strategies to realize results.

We recommend making launch events special occasions, an opportunity to signify the importance of the work of the organization and confirm the commitment of the entire leadership team.

By reviewing or recapping the Strategic Management Implementation calendar for the year you are able to establish or reinforce expectations— that implementing the strategic plan is not just a flavor of the month and is a serious organizational commitment, requiring the commitment of each and every employee.

The secret of getting ahead is getting started.

Mark Twain

4. Enhance Management and Employee Capacity

One of the essential fundamental ingredients to success is to develop management and employee capacity. Leadership separates organizations and/or departments that are successful from those that are not. Developing leadership can be developed through a combination of seminars, one-on-one executive coaching, mini leadership development moments in the planning and implementation processes, as well as through articles and books. In several leading organizations, the leadership team selects, reads, and discusses several books each year to expand their individual and collective knowledge and mindset.

Einstein said that you cannot solve a problem with the same thinking that created it. Developing leadership and employee capacity is also essential to tackling new challenges and to be more effective.

In addition to developing leadership, management, and employee capacity in a wider range of strategic thinking, business, interpersonal and technical knowledge, and skills, it is vital to develop the capacity of all staff to successfully implement plans.

5. Strengthen Individual Employee Self Leadership

Because employees are responsible for implementing their workplans day to day to achieve results, it is essential to strengthen their implementation skills and provide tools to support them. One of the most fundamental and basic tools to strengthen individual responsibility for achieving results is for all employees to use a To Do list and to schedule their major actions on a monthly and weekly basis, based on their work plans.

The late Stephen Covey, author of The Seven Habit of Highly Effective People said that it is not enough to set your priorities; in addition, you must also schedule them, block time into your calendar/ agenda.

If you don't block the time to work on them, most likely your time will be eaten up by your own or others' non important and urgent activities as well as non-important and not urgent activities.

I recommend using a software system that allows employees to monitor their own performance and update their accomplishments, reinforcing their sense of accomplishment and responsibility for results.

6. Hold Weekly One-on-One Supervisor and Employee Meetings

In high performing organizations conversations between supervisors and employees are considered a high priority. Every week, supervisors should have 15-20 minutes Check-In's with employees to discuss progress from the previous week, plans for the coming week, and discuss what support the employee needs to make continuous progress in realizing results. The Check-In meetings provide an opportunity to build trust and allow employees to discuss issues and concerns, deal with issues that might interfere with progress. In addition, in some organization's employees send a brief written report to employees; these are not a substitute for the one on-one discussions.

The one-on-one meetings provide an opportunity to review an employee's performance, strengthen supervisor-employee trust. and provide coaching in specific areas; more extensive coaching sessions should be scheduled at another time, not during Check-Ins. In most instances coaching should be scheduled separately. Quarterly meetings and monthly team meetings are not a substitute for one-on-one manager and direct report meetings.

7. Hold Monthly Management Team Meetings and Departmental Team Meetings

Monthly or bi-weekly meetings provide an opportunity for the Management Team and/or departmental teams to discuss and refresh strategic goals and priorities, operational issues, develop solutions for challenges and problems, coordinate plans and activities, and deal with a variety of organizational and/or departmental matters.

The Monthly Management Team Meetings and Departmental Team Meetings are also an opportunity for team members to update each other on progress on the Strategic Action Initiatives on which they are working. From experience I have witnessed that the departmental teams that reviewed progress on team members work plans typically accomplished their Strategic Action Initiatives, while those that did not review plans regularly accomplished far less.

8. Hold Quarterly Review Meetings

There are 3 types of Quarterly Review Sessions:

- Organizational—all departments report on progress for the past quarter. The quarterly review sessions provide a framework for accountability for results, recognition of progress, learning from what is working or may not be, and continuous improvement. In addition, the review sessions include anticipating targets and actions to achieve them in the forthcoming quarter.
- Departmental/team quarterly review of progress towards departmental or team plans. These meetings keep the team focused and on track.
- Employee—supervisory review of results for the past quarter (versus once a year), increasing their usefulness and relevance for employees and supervisors.

Hold Quarterly Milestone Meetings

A critical dimension of the implementation phase is holding "Quarterly Milestone Meetings." The purpose of these meetings is to review progress toward the quarterly and yearly targets, maintain organizational alignment, and sustain motivation towards results. At these meetings, the individual who has responsibility for each Key Success Area and its Performance Indicators:

- Reports progress against the yearly and quarterly targets with cumulative results-to-date.
- States reasons for variances and the continuous improvement plans to address them.

- Recaps their projected targets for the next quarter.
- Although an electronic dashboard allows everyone who has responsibility for a Performance Indicator to go online to report results, there is greater benefit when a management team comes together to report progress towards its targets and year- to-date.

Whether you use an electronic software tool or a simple Excel template like the one in Figure 41, below, or a simple graphic, the goal is to get a shared big picture of results to date. Quarterly meetings also strengthen management teams to work together as one unit, working for overall organizational results.

They provide for mutual accountability and allow for an expression of empathy in challenging times and to recognize and celebrate progress.

QUARTERLY REPORTING FORMAT (TARGET VS ACTUAL)								
Key Success Measures & Performance Indicators	Quarter 1		Quarter 2		Quarter 3		Quarter 4	
	Target	Actual	Target	Actual	Target	Actual	Target	Actual

Figure 43: Quarterly Reporting Format

Benefits of Quarterly Milestone Meetings

- Framework for accountability
- Keeps the implementation of plans coordinated
- Adjust strategy, as needed
- Maintain focus on priorities
- Facilitate cross functional/departmental communication
- Acknowledge progress and celebrate successes
- Reinforce and maintain commitment

Departmental Quarterly Milestone Meetings

In a similar manner, each manager should hold quarterly milestone meetings with his/her team. Departmental quarterly milestone meetings reinforce progress and maintain an emphasis on implementation of the departmental plan. When departmental teams discuss and review their work plans in their monthly and quarterly meetings, they invariably get more value out of their work plans. At the end of the year these teams have a higher level of achievement in terms of accomplishing their Strategic Action Initiatives.

Supervisory—Employee Review of Results

On the second part of the Work Plan form, right hand columns provide a space to document actual results over the past quarter while it is fresh in both the supervisor's and employee's mind, eliminating guess work at the end of the performance cycle. See Figure 42.

Q1 Expected Results (Milestone)	Q2 Expected Results (Milestone)	Q3 Expected Results (Milestone)	Q4 Expected Results (Milestone)
Status (Actual Results)	Status (Actual Results)	Status (Actual Results)	Status (Actual Results)

Figure 44: Quarterly Performance Review—Work Plan

Success doesn't happen without accountability.

> *A culture of accountability makes a*
> *good organization great and a great*
> *organization unstoppable.*

Henry J. Evans

9. Ongoing Communications & Reporting

By now it is evident that communications are a vital integrating ingredient in all and across all the Best Practices. Like implementation, communications should not be left to chance and requires a plan and a communications calendar including:

- An overview about the importance and purpose of planning
- Results/accomplishments from the past plan; lessons learned
- Outcomes of the planning session(s)
- Senior management endorsement of the plan
- Report on the Best Practices

- Announcements about the Launch sessions
- Quarterly reports

Depending on the organization and size, it may have a part to full time communications person to coordinate information to be shared in a newsletter, virtual and/or printed, special reports, radio or TV, or intranet.

10. Review and Update the Strategic Plan Annually

To keep your strategic plan current, we recommend updating your plan on an annual basis or more frequently as conditions change in your market, industry, etc.

This includes reviewing progress over the year or interim period, refining your key success measure targets for the coming year, reviewing/ updating your core strategies, establishing your priority actions for the coming year and responsibilities for each, developing action plans for the coming year so that all employees are focused and prepared for another successful year.

Chapter 13 goes more deeply into reviewing and updating your strategic plan annually.

Most organizations are complex with multiple departments, each of which has multiple Key Success goals or targets and numerous Strategic Action Initiatives for which it is accountable. Imagine for a moment a First Nation has 7 Core Strategies which each have 3 Strategic Action Initiatives for a total of 21 organizational Strategic Action Initiatives. In addition, imagine that each of its 15 department has 3 Strategic Action Initiatives for 3 of the 7 Core Strategies, resulting in another potential 315 Strategic Action Initiatives.

The good news is all 315 do not need to be done at once and will be carried out by a number of employees.

Note: In my experience not, all departments implement all the core strategies; thus, it will not have strategic actions for all Core Strategies. Nonetheless, tracking the status of all the goals/targets and Strategic Action Initiatives could easily require a part time position.

Summary

It is common knowledge that organizations do not fail in planning; rather they fail during implementation. What is required is a systematic and disciplined approach to implementation, without which the plan will fail. My goal is for organizations to successfully implement their plans to ensure they realize the future they want.

You may never know what results come of your
action, but if you do nothing there will be no result.

Mahatma Gandhi

Chapter 13: Step 7: Annual Strategic Plan Review & Update

Keeping your plan current

Thinking is easy. Acting is difficult.
To put one's thoughts
into action is the most difficult thing is the world.

Goethe

Many metaphors describe the importance of reviewing and updating your strategic plan, e.g., we have come to the end of our journey, learn from the past to avoid making the same mistakes, taking stock, etc.

It is tempting to charge ahead planning for the next year without pausing to review the past year, missing the opportunity to discern valuable lessons about your plans, what was accomplished or not, why or why not, what did you learn from that, and the ongoing implementation of your plan.

In conversations with several organizations, I have discovered that they do not review and update their strategic plans. Once their plan is developed, it is filed away without an implementation system, including the Annual Strategic Plan Review and Updates. As a result, they lose valuable insights, plans to achieve them go unrealized, and they do not gain momentum. Many good strategic plans are 'still born', never given life. Or, at best, only live a short time with a few actions taken, consequently the plan is forgotten.

Strategic management expert, Stephen Haines, recommends keeping your strategic plan up and successfully running year after year, as a strategic management system, after the newness has born off. You will need to conduct a yearly follow-up to diagnose the overall success of your implementation. The review and update will provide you an opportunity for continuous improvements of your plan and the implementation process, complimenting the internal Quarterly Reviews of your plan and its progress.

Although most organizations have a yearly independent financial audit, an annual independent audit of the strategic management is rarely done and not advocated in management literature or on the radar of boards of directors.

What to Include and Goals

According to Haines, the Annual Strategic Review and Update should include a review and assessment feedback report with recommendations from an external, unbiased perspective on your organization's strategy implementation. He suggests the assessment process concerns two goals:

1. Assess the status of the Strategic Plan achievement
2. Assess the Strategic Management Process itself

It is vital to focus on both goals, as they are interdependent. The result of the update should be the following four outcomes:

1. Laying the foundation for updating your Strategic Plan
2. Clarifying and updating your annual planning and strategic budgeting priorities for the next year.

3. Problem-solving any issues raised in assessing either of the two goals above.
4. Re-setting next year's comprehensive strategic management calendar.

Two-Step Assessment Process

Step 1: Assessment

Yearly Assessment Data Collection may include areas such as:

*   conduct interviews with leaders and senior management
*   conduct focus groups with employees and supervisors
*   conduct interviews with board members, suppliers, members, clients, etc.
*   review of strategic management documents, e.g., notes from quarterly meetings, etc.
*   review agendas of change processes and meeting outcomes
*   review group meeting notes from supervisors and employees, and stakeholders
*   review survey data

This data provides valuable feedback and insights to determine what is working well and areas for potential improvement.

I have used an assessment process through a review meeting with organizational and divisional teams. Each division carried out an assessment using the same framework of its past year and reported to the whole organizational team using a similar reporting format which included:

*   Assessment of their past year - identifying accomplishments and reporting their 'Prouds'*, what they were proud of, important achievements of the

year, and 'Sorries'*, which had not gone as planned. From their assessment, what they had learned, and reported.

- They also decided on a theme for the past year and depicted it creatively, e.g., music, drawing, short skit, etc. One of the more memorable ones is that they worked together like a beehive.
- Additionally, they reported how the strategic management system had supported their departmental work and how they would strengthen it in the next fiscal year.

*The terms Prouds and Sorries were created by Marvin Weisbord, author of Future Search.

- After hearing all divisional reports, we synthesized:

  - Key 'Prouds' and accomplishments and 'Sorries' of the past year for the organization
  - Overall learnings
  - An overall metaphor or theme for the organization for the past fiscal year
  - Learning about the Strategic Management system

Step 2: Updating the Strategic Plan

Building on the assessment and review, we then updated the strategic plan, including the following ABCDE tasks:

- Reviewing and refreshing the purpose, mission, and vision, what evidence of progress have they seen the organization is making towards each. Checked values in terms of which values they saw in action which ones needs more attention in the coming year.

- Reporting on emerging future environmental trends likely to impact the organization.
- Reporting on progress towards the overall key success measure and key performance indicators (KPI s) and targets. Reflected on whether or not they were the most important to monitor and on which to report. Confirmed and reestablished KPI targets.
- Refreshing and updating the SWOT analysis.
- Reviewing progress towards the Strategic and the Strategic Action Initiatives for the plan for the year, identifying if Action Initiative was: Completed, In progress, rescheduled for the next year, or should be Deleted.

The Organizational Strategic Plan report was updated, and each division updated its strategic plan for the coming fiscal year, serving as a roadmap for the coming year.

Checklist for Reviewing and Updating Your Strategic Plan

- Assess progress towards the plan – accomplishments, challenges, and lessons learned
- Identify future environment trends likely to impact your organization so that you can proactively take advantage of opportunities and minimize threats
- Review and refresh the purpose, mission, and vision, and values
- Update your key performance indicators targets/goals for the coming planning cycle and year
- Update your strategies/objectives to close the gaps between where you want to be and are today
- Keep your plan agile, responsive so that you can quickly address issues and opportunities that emerge

Recap of Key Points

- Conduct a yearly follow-up and independent assessment of your organization's performance regarding your plan's successful implementation and the Strategic Management System, the key to *making it work*.
- It is a rolling plan, recycle and update it annually your strategic plan and all its components, reviewing the entire ABCDE model.
- Haines says, *take the time to do it right.* Usually, however, it takes about a third of the time.
- Excellence is doing 10,000 little things right on an ongoing basis, and the Strategic Management System is about continual improvement in executing your plan.

Chapter 14.
Strategic Management System
Putting it all together

Throughout this book, you have been learning how to achieve three goals:

Goal 1: Develop strategic and annual plans and documents
Goal 2: Ensure a successful rollout, implementation, and change
Goal 3: Build and sustain high performance over the long term

Together, they create a Strategic Management System which includes Planning + Implementation + Change + Leadership

A Strategic Management System is a comprehensive system to lead, manage and change one's total organization, in a well-planned, and integrated fashion based on your strategies to develop and successfully achieve your desired future vision.

Figure 45: Yearly Strategic Management Cycle
Used with permission, Haines Centre for Strategic Management

The real value of the systems model is not the A, B, C, D, E phases, or the 7 progressive steps. It is the circular nature of the system, based on systems thinking. It can be visualized as a Yearly Strategic Management Cycle Figure 42, above.

The five-phase Systems Thinking Approach enables you to tailor your planning approach to your current situation. The good news is you can begin the process at any of its five A, B, C, D, E phases. If your organization already has a mission and vision, and values statements, you can begin your planning process by developing your Key Success Measures and continue from there.

Alternatively, if you have completed a Current State Assessment and already have developed your strategies, you can develop the full planning process for 3-year plan or cascade the plan with its strategies to Departmental Planning (Level 3). The circular process offers 5 options to get started.

One of the major benefits of the Systems Thinking Approach is its flexibility which can be tailored to your organization's situation and needs. Additionally, the ABCDE model can be applied to diverse applications, e.g., economic development, health care, housing, literally all aspects and functions of a community or organization.

Commitment to the ongoing implementation of the Strategic Management System is essential to achieve desired results on an ongoing basis.

Just because we cannot see clearly the end of the road, there is no reason for not seeing out on the essential journey. On the contrary, great change, dominates the world, and unless we move with change, we will become its victims.

John F. Kennedy

Section 3:

Developing and Human and Organizational Capacity

Chapter 15:
Leadership Commitment
The essential factor

Leadership is vital in successfully developing your strategic and operational plan and is essential to the entire process from beginning to end. If senior leadership is not committed to the planning process and the final plan, you can be sure no one else will be. Leadership sets the tone. To quote, Kouves and Posner, *"Leadership must model the way."* Indeed, leadership does model the way. A leader's commitment is transparent whether they want it to be or not.

> *"Leadership is practiced not so much in*
> *words as in attitude and in actions.*

Harold S. Geneen

One of my favorite examples of leadership comes from the story and movie, The Polar Express. In the story, children take an imaginary train bound for the North Pole to visit Santa. They experience various perils on their trip, and each of the main characters exhibits different characteristics. As they neared their homes, each had their tickets punched with a keyword reflecting their journey. One learned Humility, another to Believe, and another Leadership - who set direction, took risks, and cared for others.

What leadership is needed to Develop and Implement a Strategic Plan?

In working with many organizations over the years, I have had the pleasure of partnering with some extraordinary leaders committed to the strategic management process who took leadership. I had also known others who did not. From research and experience, the ten critical leadership characteristics that are essential to strategic planning and implementation include:

- Not Satisfied with the Status Quo
- Building Bridges to the Future
- Being Future Focused
- Engaging Others
- Committing to the Planning and Implementation Process
- Being Strategic Thinkers
- Challenging Others
- Recognizing the Importance of a Systematic Approach
- Holding Others Accountable
- Following-through

Not Satisfied with the Status Quo

Great leaders are never satisfied with status quo, static thinking, conventional wisdom, or everyday performance. According to Mike Myatt, a contributor to Forbes Magazine, leadership is a pursuit of excellence, what's next, change value, results, relationships, service, knowledge, and something bigger than themselves. The best leaders are simply uncomfortable with anything that embraces the status quo.

Wise leaders understand it's not just enough to seek—pursuit of excellence must be intentional, focused, consistent, aggressive, and unyielding. It is essential to pursue the right things for the right reasons. A leader can't do it alone—it is vital to enlist others in the pursuit, to collaborate with others.

A word of caution against trivial pursuits—don't confuse intent with simple goal setting. Outcomes are important, but what happens after results are achieved. Nothing tells the world more about a leader than what they pursue—that which you seek is that which you value. You can wax eloquent all you like, but your actions will ultimately reveal what you truly value.

Build Bridges to the Future

More than anything else, leaders build bridges to the future—bridges that help their teams, organizations, and communities move from where they are to where they need to be.

Joel Barker, the creator of the movie Leadershift and author of Paradigms, uses a bridge metaphor to show that leaders forge a new path to the future. Bridges made of hope, ideas, and opportunity; bridges wide and strong enough so that all who wish to cross can do so safely.

These bridges are necessary to grow and thrive in an ever-changing world. Barker helps us understand that leaders must take responsibility for the bridges they build and the impact those bridges will have on the future. He encourages leaders to construct bridges to the future so that they're wide enough and strong enough for those who choose to follow us.

Future Focused

To build bridges to the future, leaders need to be open to new ways of doing things, building on past accomplishments, and are not satisfied with the status quo. Barker says that the future is the place to which leaders lead others. It is the leader's responsibility to take care of tomorrow. Stephen Haines noted that leaders have two responsibilities, planning for tomorrow and ensuring that today's business is also taken care of.

A leader's primary responsibility is to focus on the future, while a follower's primary responsibility is to focus on today, carrying out the critical activities that keep the organization running from day-to-day. Future-focused leaders shift their thinking from "doing it all" to allowing others to contribute to the group's progress.

Engages Others

A leader is someone you choose to follow to a place you wouldn't go by yourself. There are two critical components of this definition, according to Barker. The first is choice—you choose to follow this person; it is always the follower's decision. The second component has to do with the place you are going to. This place requires the leader to go first and lead the way. It has a feeling of risk, uncertainty, of trying something new or different. That's why the follower won't go by alone.

One of the leaders I have worked with commits the organization to invest time and energy to update its strategic and operational plan annually. One year some of the management team resisted the idea of updating the plan annually.

Acknowledging their concerns, the Executive Director reminded them updating their strategic plan annually ensures that every employee in the organization knows where they are going, how they will get there, and their role in making it happen. In addition, they agreed on improvements to the process and created a schedule to update the plan for the coming year. Without the commitment of the leader to having an up-to-date road map for the year ahead, nothing would happen. He realized the value of everyone in the organization being prepared for the year early and clarifying their strategic priorities.

The follower must willingly choose to follow the leader. A leader who forces others into compliance is nothing more than a tyrant. A true leader earns the respect and trust needed for people to follow them, even in adverse or risky situations. The focus and vision of the leader enable them to believe and trust that the outcome will be greater than the risk. In the same organization mentioned previously, employees value hearing the leader's direction who inspires them.

Successful leaders use the power of vision to help them build bridges to the future. Vision is an essential leadership tool, helping people and organizations outperform their assets. Barker says it does not matter whether your organization is a not-for-profit, a corporation, a hospital, or a nation—everyone benefits from having a powerful vision of the future. A shared vision is the single most potent component for building bridges to the future.

Compelling visions have common characteristics:

- Shared by everyone in the organization
- Positive and supports the community

Tewatohnhi'saktha has a profound vision:

> *a self-sufficient community that fosters quality*
> *of life for Kanien'kehaka ne Kahnawa'kehro:*
> *non and creates collective prosperity for future*
> *generations consistent with our cultural values.*

The Board of Directors, managers, and employees supporting the vision have the passion and commitment to continue to turn their vision into action to realize results. It is no longer a vision or far-off goal but a successful, working reality.

Vision is equally important to engage followers in not-for-profit and for-profit organizations. In their book Built to Last, Jim Collins and Jerry Porras share the example that one dollar invested in a visionary company will yield six times the return of its non-visionary competitor. The visionary company will do fifteen times better than the overall stock market.

In the past and throughout much of history, leaders created a vision and handed it down to their followers. Today, we know that such an approach doesn't work—people are more informed, educated, want to use their skills, and knowledge to contribute to the vision.

The new way of thinking about vision recognizes that the larger community or organization needs to have a hand in creating it. Creating the vision together allows for shared meaning and understanding of the vision by all followers.

Commitment to the Planning and Implementation Process

At another organization with whom I worked, a president arbitrarily decided how long the planning would take and further reduced the time while still expecting them to produce a quality plan. Although he recognized that the company needed to focus its direction for the future and establish a growth plan, he undervalued planning and the process required to develop it. Without a commitment to the whole planning process, energy had to be re-invested repeatedly to move the process forward, causing delays. The lesson learned—the time allotted to planning reflects the leader's value of planning.

I was requested to make a half-day strategic planning overview with another Indigenous Chief and Council. Before the presentation, I learned the time for my presentation had been reduced from half a day to an hour and a half—in reflection, this was an early indicator that planning was not a high priority for them.

During the presentation, I asked the councilors to identify how important it was for them to develop a plan for their future. Most councilors rated the need for change and developed a plan as high. To assist in carrying out the planning process, they hired a part-time project coordinator who was also involved in many other projects and was spread very thin. He formed a planning committee composed of community members representing various organizations. Unfortunately, many committee members were not influential with leadership in their organizations.

On the day of the planning session, only one of the councilors showed up. Even though the council had endorsed the planning process authorizing the investment, they had not bought into it, as evidenced by their absence from the process.

In retrospect, I should have asked two more questions in my earlier meeting with them: "Will you participate in the planning process? Are you committed to developing and implementing a plan for the community?"

Resistance to change was more significant than a desire for a better future. Surface the concerns of decision-makers by having individual interviews with them before meeting them as a group. I would have gained insight into their concerns and better at addressing them.

We recognize that people support that which they help to create. When participation is low, so is commitment. Although community members from many sectors developed a good plan, it was not the council's plan which they did not endorse. I share this to illustrate why vital leadership commitment is crucial from start to finish.

The lesson that emerged from this experience points to some of the common mistakes in planning. The sole goal of some leaders is to develop a plan or have a planning session event at an offsite location. They may have low expectations about planning, believing that nothing ever happens with plans anyway. Such an attitude likely becomes a self-fulfilling prophecy.

Leaders who want more than the status quo build bridges to the future, engaging their organizational teams in developing and successfully implementing plans. Einstein said it well, *"Things are the way they are because someone wants them that way."*

Before commencing with strategic planning, it is crucial to:

- Verify leadership's views about planning and implementation of the plan
- Determine the issues they want the plan to deal with and the pain they want to reduce
- Establish the outcomes that they want to achieve, their level of commitment
- Determine their willingness to be involved in the planning

- Establish their expectations for implementing the plan
- Create a realistic time frame and schedule for the process
- Establish the resources available for the implementation of the plan, and
- Develop clarity about what is required to implement the plan successfully.

Strategic Thinkers

One essential leadership characteristic is the ability to think strategically, including thinking ahead 3- 5 years into the future, anticipating trends likely to impact the organization, and being able to position the organization relative to its competitor's services and products. It is also essential to develop alternative scenarios and strategies to close the gap between where they want to be in the future and where they are now. Additionally, to test that strategies will achieve the desired-future results. Equally important, to keep their strategies alive through ongoing conversation.

According to a survey of 151 companies conducted by McKinsey and Company and published in the article, *"Creating More Value with Corporate Strategy"*, managers of the best organizations spend more than 15% of their time on strategy on an ongoing basis over a year. *How much time do leaders in your organization spend on planning?*

Challenge the Thinking of Others

Closely related to being strategic thinkers, they also challenge the thinking of others, and they stretch their followers' thinking to the next level. Time and time again, I witnessed the difference it made when a leader who thinks strategically challenges followers' thinking. Although it took time, what emerged was a higher level of thinking and more strategic ideas.

In addition, influential leaders recognize the potential of their employees, challenging them to do better to bring out their greatness, allowing them to discover their abilities. Although it may not be easy for employees to change their thinking in the short term, in the long term, they appreciate having had a leader who will help them to become more and to discover their real potential.

Recognizes the Importance of a Systematic Approach

Because they are in it for the long term, these leaders recognize the importance of implementing a systematic approach for achieving consistent results on an ongoing basis, not just the flavor of the month. I must admit such leaders are rare. I have met leaders who are happy with the status quo, those who gave up quickly in the face of resistance from a few employees who did not want to do more, ones who focus only on the top 13% of the Iceberg for Change and those who recognize that systems and processes are needed to achieve consistent long-term results.

These leaders ensure organizational policies and procedures align with their strategic plans, structured to support the strategic direction. Each department and its employees align with the organizational strategic and operational plans. They are the leaders who don't bat an eye, recognizing the importance of a systematic implementation process to ensure the ongoing, timely execution of plans. They review other organizational systems, such as Human Resources, Financial Systems, and Information Technology, to align and support the organizational strategy.

Holds Others Accountable

Because they are results-focused, these leaders recognize the importance of holding themselves and others accountable. They make sure employees are clear about their accountabilities, expected results, have action plans with target dates. They expect the best from their employees and peers. Most of the time, they get it. They review performance regularly with individuals and their teams and provide regular feedback. Accountability is real, not just a fluffy term. These accountabilities are built into the strategic management process as well as the performance management process.

> *If we can't make and keep commitments*
> *to ourselves and others, our*
> *commitments become meaningless.*

Stephen Covey

Follow-through

Many leaders are good at starting things but not good at following through. Not because they don't care—they get busy with other priorities and concerns. Dropped or delayed plans and projects often convey a message to employees that the leader is not committed to the strategic and operational plan. Leaders need to be on top of their commitments and follow up with employees and teams about their commitments. Failure to follow up sends a message that the plan and its strategic actions are not important. Similarly, it conveys to employees that their efforts don't matter.

The ideas to successfully implement your plan, described in Chapter 12, are designed to assist you with following through to get results and honor your employees as vital human assets.

Best leadership practices to support planning and implementation:

- Set a clear context for why and how planning is vital for the organization
- Model the way—provide a visible commitment to the process
- Actively participate in the planning process
- Commit to the whole strategic management process and scheduling it:
  - starting with the plan-to-plan session
  - holding the planning process sessions
  - developing work plans
  - developing strategic budgets
  - carrying out a final review of the plans
  - ensuring that resources are in place to implement the strategic plan priorities
  - holding quarterly review
  - reviewing and updating the strategic plan annually.
- Create Strategic Action Initiatives to realize the strategies to close the gaps between the desired future and current situation
- Put in place a systematic process to monitor results
- Recognize people's efforts
- Repeatedly remind people why planning is essential
- Keep the vision alive day after day by talking about it in conversations and meetings

The best leaders pursue being better leaders. They know that failing in this pursuit is nothing short of guaranteeing they'll be replaced by those who don't.

Mike Myatt

Chapter 16:
Aligning Your Organization

*Systems, processes & culture to
support your strategic plan*

Many organizations concentrate on goals in their planning and have 'Content Myopia.' As the Iceberg Theory of Change, Figure 44, below, illustrates, they focus their efforts on the 13% above the water while ignoring that successful change depends on the processes, structures, and organizational culture, competencies, and resources in place to achieve their desired goals. Overlooking the 87% results is a severe and costly mistake.

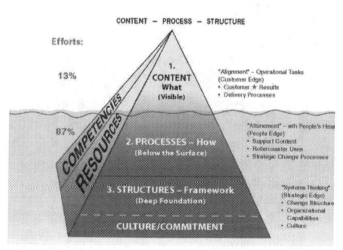

Figure 46: Iceberg Theory of Change
Used with permission, Haines Centre for Strategic Management

Achieving results requires more than setting goals and determining the actions to implement them. The Iceberg Theory of Change illustrates that an organization must also put in place and update the internal processes, systems needed to achieve wanted results.

Additionally, it must ensure its organizational culture (the way things get done in the workplace) supports its plan. Their plan must include developing employees' competencies to achieve the results they seek and provide the needed resources to be effective.

Designing, building, and sustaining a member-focused, high-performance learning organization requires a balance in how organizations spend their time and energy between:

1. The Content (goals, tasks) and focus of the organization
2. The Processes and systems—how tasks are carried out
3. The Infrastructure within which the content and processes operate

Identifying Misalignments

The first step to improving internal alignment is to determine the one or two systems that will provide the best return on investment in both time and money. Because we believe that those who work in the organization know it best, we recommend engaging them in assessing the organization and identifying misalignments with the strategy.

We recently assessed an organization's readiness to embark on a community planning process. Using Raven's Creating Results Scorecard, the assessment revealed a low level of readiness to engage in a comprehensive community planning process without developing the processes, systems, and culture needed to achieve them. Figure 47, below.

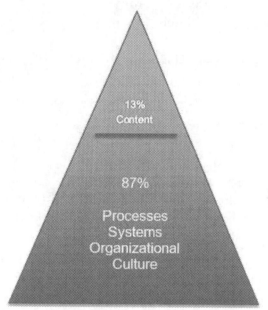

Figure 47: Example–Organizational Readiness for Change

Example- Organizational Readiness for Change Based on the Iceberg Theory of Change

Content - 13% of Efforts

XYFN leadership desires for their community:

- Greater variety of businesses
- Expanded housing and home ownership
- Expanded education and training
- Expanded health facilities and services
- Expanded community facilities and services
- Expanded sports and recreation facilities and programs
- Expanded financial base

- Expanded accessibility outside community
- Strong Cree culture
- Clean and safe community
- Caring for the environment

To realize the Content above the line, **87% of efforts** need to be focused on areas below the iceberg surface. The percentages for each reflect XYFN's current level of capability from the Scorecard assessment.

Processes

- Up-to-date strategic and operational plan – Av. 1.0
- Clear direction and a shared vision for our future – Av. 2.4
- An effective systematic process to track results – Av. 2.5
- Reaching our goals – Av. 3.19
- Effectively using our time and money – Av. 3.0
- Update to date policies and procedures – Not assessed

Systems

- Aligned at all levels of the organization – Av. 2.6
- Function as a high-performance organization – Av. 2.2
- System for establishing priorities & tracking results – Av. 1.0
- Integrated performance management system – Av. 1.0

Culture Organizational

- Focused and proactive – Av. 2.2
- Organizational culture aligned with organizational goals – Av. 2.5

- Staff is highly engaged – Av. 3.0
- Collaborative, team-oriented, aligned to shared vision – not assessed

What is your organization's readiness for planning and implementation?

Aligning Processes

Organizations are composed of thousands of processes. A process is a sequenced set of activities that produce a result. If an organization is not running smoothly, likely it has process problems or misaligned systems. It could also be that the organization is missing processes, like as shown in the above example; or it may be that the processes are not being executed effectively. Many organizations do not know how effective their internal processes are based on measurable data. A starting point for such organizations is to begin by making a list of their processes, assessing their effectiveness, and establishing priorities for improvement that will have the most significant impact.

One organization with whom we worked was not meeting its targets; in assessing the situation, one of their issues was a breakdown in hand-offs between departments, resulting in delays in shipping products to customers.

Processes are like blueprints that describe how an organization works. Mapping out the processes allows a team to establish how things are currently performed, identifying areas for improvement, often reducing the time required to complete the process while increasing their effectiveness. With a department that provides access to training and employment counseling, we mapped out their current processes. Areas of misalignment were identified and a gap in post-training support processes was identified. The emphasis had been on getting people enrolled in training but not on post-training support to help them secure employment.

Effective processes have the following characteristics:

- Well defined, have a clear intent
- Transferrable to others to execute
- Repeatable, specific steps
- Flexible, allowing for future changes
- Measurable, measuring output, lag measures

It is crucial to get the actual people who execute the process involved in defining and changing it, as they are the ones who understand how things work and the allowable exceptions.

How would you rate the effectiveness of the processes of your organization? Which require the most improvement?

Aligning Policies

A policy is a rule that guides the operation of an organization, providing consistency across its departments and functions. Many years ago, I was an employee of a major financial institution with a rulebook. Rules were added to reduce the likelihood of similar errors being repeated. At that time, the book was nearly two feet tall. I have always wondered just how tall the rulebook might be now! Although policies and processes are different, they are interrelated.

Formal policies should only be created when they will truly add value. It is important to create the critical few rules versus the many. An organization can have aligned processes and misaligned policies or vice versa. Policies often become outdated and need to be updated to serve clients' or citizens' needs in today's world.

Example:

A well-implemented policy has the following characteristics:

- It is necessary—it helps people to do their job more effectively
- Clear intent—the reason underlying the policy is clear and means the same thing to all employees
- The intent of the policy is honored by the person implement it who has the freedom and aptitude for adjusting its implementation to meet the intended reasons
- It is aligned—the policy supports the organization's goals
- It is measurable— results can be measured
- Policies are short, simple, and easy to interpret
- Policies are flexible—provide the reason behind them and give employees the freedom to adapt them to the situations

How would you rate the effectiveness of the policies of your organization? Which require the most improvement?

Aligning Systems

Most organizations have numerous systems, ranging from information technology systems, human resources systems, financial systems, service delivery systems, to name only a few. As well, its departments have systems, i.e., housing, emergency preparedness, etc. A system is a set of components that work together for the overall objective of the whole.

The most distinctive feature of any system, according to Stephen Haines, is that every part influences and affects every other part of the same system. Ideally, all parts of a system work together synergistically. Furthermore, no individual part is independent of the others.

The characteristics of a true system include:

- The whole is primary, and the parts are secondary
- Each system functions uniquely—each system has properties/ functions that none of the parts can do individually
- System purpose first; parts support the whole, playing their role considering the purpose for which the whole system exists
- All parts are interdependent—parts, elements, subsystems are interdependent
- Systems cannot be subdivided into independent parts; a system cannot function effectively when it loses a part
- Small changes produce big results—change in any element of a system affects the whole and other elements or subsystems. According to Haines, small changes can produce big results, if the leverage points are clear.

How would you rate the effectiveness of the systems of your organization? Which require the most improvement?

Organizational Culture

In recent years, the awareness of the impact of organizational culture has dramatically increased as an essential differentiator between organizations. Culture is the way things are done in an organization - the accepted way people behave and how they interact with others. For example, do they show up on time or not?

Value, keeping commitments. Readily assist other team members, or is individual achievement more highly valued? Acknowledge the achievements of others? Share credit for work, and so on? Culture matters—an organization's culture either supports or inhibits achieving results and realizing its desired future.

When the organizational culture is non-supportive of its strategy:

- Opportunities are missed
- Employees are disengaged
- Expected results do not happen

Competencies

According to research, finding talented workers is one of the biggest factors limiting growth. There is a mismatch between required talents and those available. Therefore, an organization can either search for talented employees or develop the competencies they need internally.

When an organization is growing or venturing in new directions, employees must have the competencies to succeed. Competencies, a combination of knowledge and skills, are acquired in various ways. These could include hands-on experience, coaching on the job, or mentoring, where knowledge and skills are passed down from one generation to the next. Also, competencies can be acquired through in-house or external courses, seminars, online courses, and special assignments.

To ensure that an organization has the competencies needed at the right time, it is vital to develop human resources and succession plans forecasting the competencies needed 5- 7 years in the future. An organization can systematically develop and update the knowledge and skills of its employees. Or, it can selectively recruit or hire employees with specialized competencies who might also assist in training other employees to develop their knowledge and skills. Employee training and development is one of the most vital investment an organization can make to build performance capability and growth.

- *What competencies are most needed now in your organization?*
- *Which ones will be needed in the future?*
- *What is the priority for development?*

Resources

In addition to competencies to perform, employees also require the right resources at the right time to achieve results. Resources are the equipment, supplies, and necessary support to carry out their jobs and be successful. These include the basics such as a phone, computer, software, paper, files, specialized tools, equipment, etc.

What is more challenging is providing the support employees need to carry out the tasks, including time to work on Strategic Action Initiatives and access to others who are vital to accomplishing results.

- *What resources does your organization need to develop and implement a strategic plan?*
- *Where and how can you access the needed resources?*

No matter how carefully you plan your goals,
they will never be more than pipe dreams
unless you pursue them with gusto.

SW. Clement Stone 1902-2002,

Chapter 17: Building A High-Performance Organization

Achieves results day-after-day

Developing your strategic and operational plan is estimated to get you 20% of the way towards your desired future and results. Successfully implementing your plan and monitoring progress achieves another 40%. The final 40% is achieved by building a high-performance organization achieving results, and performing at high-level day-to-day, year-to-year.

A leader's job is to investigate the future and see the organization not as it is but as it can be.

Jim Rohn

Today most organizations experience tremendous pressure to meet and exceed customer/ client and stakeholder expectations, deliver quality products and services at competitive prices, and deliver a high level of service—often with reduced funding.

You may be wondering what is meant by "a high-performance organization." Why be one, and what are the benefits of being one? What key factors contribute to high performance? How does an organization build and sustain a high-performance culture and workplace?

Allow me to answer those questions one by one.

What Is A High-Performance Organization?

There are many definitions of what constitutes a high-performance organization (HPO) and what is required to be one.

There is, however, no one single factor that makes an organization high-performing—that is, an organization that consistently achieves results. The core of the definitions is understanding that the most important factor driving growth and contributing to overall results *is people*. Moreover, there is a growing recognition of the need to create the kind of organization that allows employees to function in which they do their best, which sets the stage for establishing a high-performance organization.

> *The greatest lesson I've learned is that*
> *people have a more significant impact on*
> *growth or success than anything else.*

Jim Stewart

In the past several decades, organizations worldwide have been searching for the elements that constitute continuous organizational success. Fueled by bestsellers such as *In Search Of Excellence* and *Good to Great*, managers have tried many different improvement concepts, often with mixed results. These studies aimed to identify factors that determine the continuous success of high-performance organizations.

An analysis of 280 research studies of high performance identified 35 characteristics of an HPO. These were subsequently used in a large financial service case study to identify its HPO status and the improvements needed to become a genuinely excellent organization. The study results show it is possible to identify factors that determine continuous organizational success.

The concept of a high-performance organization evolved from research into the link between human resource management and organizational performance.

According to Leigh Goessl, an HPO concentrates on bringing out the best in people and designs itself to produce sustainable results. An HPO balances the needs of its internal and external stakeholders, those with interest in the organization.

A Yale University study, summarized in a report by the Ken Blanchard Companies, identified six core HPO elements, including:

- Shared information and open communication
- Compelling vision
- Ongoing learning
- Relentless focus on results
- Energizing systems and structures
- Shared power and high involvement

Each is described briefly below:

Shared Information and Open Communication
High-performing organizations have a broad definition of what is relevant and necessary information. Moreover, the information needed to make informed decisions is readily available to employees.

Compelling Vision
The organization's vision, and its purpose and values, are clearly understood and passionately supported by employees

at all levels, resulting in a highly focused culture that drives desired organizational results.

Ongoing Learning

In an HPO, there is a constant focus on improving employee capabilities through training and development, increasing knowledge and skills, and transferring personnel throughout the organization.

Relentless Focus on Results

One of the earmarks of an HPO is its focus on producing outstanding results. More specifically, they focus on results from the perspective of the customer.

Energizing Systems and Structures

In addition to purpose, mission, vision, and goals, an organization needs systems, structures, and processes that support high performance, making it easier for people to get their jobs done.

Shared Power and High Involvement

In high-performance organizations, power and decision-making are distributed throughout the organization and not restricted to the top of the hierarchy. Instead, participation and teamwork are a way of life throughout the organization by providing cross training to expand employee's capabilities. A literature search conducted by Marco Schreurs, a cofounder of Direction, Briefings for Business Leaders Europe BV (est. 1999), and the Center for Organizational Performance, identified five success factors that determine what makes an organization a High-Performance Organization.

Success factors of an organization that achieves better financial and non-financial results than comparable organizations over at least five to ten years are:

- Quality of Management
- Openness and Action Orientation
- Long Term Orientation
- Continuous Improvement
- High-Quality Workforce

Quality of Management

Management capability in HPOs is high and dedicated to building relationships based on trust by combining integrity and coaching with highly exemplary behavior. As well, managers in HPO are quick to make decisions (also regarding non-performers), are results-oriented, and are committed to the organization's long-term vision.

Quality of Employees

HPO employees are diverse, complementary, and capable of working together well. They are flexible and resilient when it comes to achieving results. Every day they are busy answering the question, "How can I make our organization more successful?"

Openness and Action Orientation

The culture of an HPO is an open one in which everyone is involved in essential processes through dialogue, continuous sharing of knowledge, learning from mistakes, where change is encouraged, and action is taken to improve performance.

Continuous Improvement and Innovation

High-Performance Organizations are committed to continuous improvement and innovation. Leaders and employees continuously simplify, align, and renew processes, services, and products.

Long-Term Orientation

To an HPO, continuity in the long term always takes precedence over profit in the short term. The long-term orientation of an HPO applies to clients, collaboration partners, and relationships with employees. Management positions are filled by employees from within the organization whenever possible.

Note: When strategy and management quality are compared, the latter proves far more critical to the success of an organization. A team of good people can achieve anything it wants, while an organization with a clear and well-defined strategy but lacking the right people to execute it is bound to go nowhere. On the other hand, as described in Chapter 7, the account of the Fortune 500 division illustrated that a reactive, unfocused, and misaligned team of talented people is not likely to be high performers.

Best Practices Research

According to the research of the Aberdeen Group on Creating a High-Performance Culture, managing employee performance can provide significant results when done well. Without the full support of their supervisors, employee growth and development will be less effective.

Aberdeen's Best Practices for Creating a High-Performance Culture recommend:

- Creating a mindset about the importance of performance management
- Supervisors must have a clear understanding of the value and importance of employee performance management
- Developing employee's capability and performance as a core responsibility for which they are held accountable
- Providing software to support planning, weekly and daily priorities, and track and report on progress
- Increase the frequency of formal and informal performance conversations.

Using software makes it easier to monitor progress for the whole organization and or by a specific department or employee or by a core strategy or specific strategic action initiatives.

Frequent performance conversations are vital to keeping employees abreast of progress informally and openly. The more employees know about their performance results and how it affects organizational results, the better they are likely to do, and so too will the company.

The Benefits of Being a High-Performance Organization

According to Epstein, HPO's have strong financial results, satisfied customers and employees, high levels of individual initiative, increased productivity, and innovation, aligned performance measurement, reward systems, and strong leadership. A high-performance organization achieves financial and non-financial results better than those of its peer group over at least five to ten years (Waal, 2006, 2007).

Financial Results of HPO's Compared with Those of Non-HPO's

- Revenue Growth +10%
- Profitability +29%
- Return on Assets (ROA) +7%
- Return on Equity (ROE) +17%
- Return on Investment (ROI) +20%
- Return on Sales (ROS) +11%
- Total Shareholder Return +23%

The HPO study shows a direct relationship between the HPO factors and competitive performance. Organizations that pay more attention to HPO factors score higher on these, consistently achieve better results than their peers in every industry, sector, and country in the world.

Conversely, the opposite is true; organizations that score low on HPO factors rank at the bottom of their industry in performance levels. The difference between HPO's and non-HPO's is particularly significant in the case of Long-term Commitment—HPO's pay considerably more attention to the designated aspects of a long-term commitment than non-HPO organizations. Therefore, they are able to improve their performance significantly.

How to Build and Sustain A High-Performance Culture and Workplace

You may be feeling your organization should strive to be a High-Performance Organization, but where do you start? Just as there is no one 'silver bullet' or single factor that will transform your organization into an HPO, nor is there one single place to start. If you have systematically carried out the steps described in previous chapters, you are already well on your way to being an HPO.

To accelerate becoming a High Performance Organization, using the HPO factors, develop and implement an action plan to enhance high performance.

One of my HPO clients carries out an Employee Satisfaction Survey every two years. The survey assesses employee perceptions about 20 work-related factors, which correlate with the HPO factors listed in this chapter. Conduct the survey anonymously to encourage candid responses. Report the results to the whole organization, your divisions, and manager and non-manager groups. The HPO type of survey will provide valuable information to identify which HPO factors will be most beneficial to strengthen human and organizational performance.

Use the survey results as your benchmark and re-survey in another year or two to assess your progress.

This same client then uses the survey results to plan and carry out various initiatives to increase employee satisfaction in areas requiring improvement. Between carrying out the complete HPO survey, my client conducts mini pulse surveys to assess progress in the areas targeted for improvement and makes strategic investments to sustain itself as a High-Performance Organization.

> *Create a place where strong performers*
> *want to be employed.*

Author unknown.

7-Step Checklist to Create Your Future

The checklist below is designed as a job aid to assist you in keeping track of your progress throughout the Annual Planning Cycle.

Step	Action	Done
1. Environmental Scan	Assign individual employees with responsibility to research trends for each SKEPTIC factor	
	Research SKEPTIC factor trends	
	Identify impacts of trends	
	Identify trends that are most likely to occur and would have a high impact	
2. Desired Future Vision	Develop/review the Purpose /Mission Statement	
	Envision/refresh the desired future	
	Articulate/review the Core Values	
	Create Rallying Cry	
3. Establish Feedback Process	Identify Key Success Measures (KSM)	
	Develop Key Performance Indicators for each KSM	
	Establish benchmarks for each KPI	
	Set year 1, 2, 3 and quarterly targets for each KPI	
4. Assess Current State	Identify strengths and actions to build on each	
	Identify weaknesses and actions to minimize each	
	Identify opportunities and actions to seize each	
	Identify threats and actions to reduce each	
	Summarize the most important strengths, weaknesses, opportunities, and threats	

Figure 48: 7 Steps Checklist to Create Your Future

Step	Action	Done
5. Develop Core Strategies	Group actions from Current State Assessment into major 5-7 core strategies	
	Develop a statement of intent for each core strategy	
	Create 3-5 key strategic actions initiatives for each core strategy	
	Determine the year each strategic action initiative would be implemented, e.g., year 1, 2, 3	
	Decide who will have Lead Accountability for each strategic action initiative	
6. Implement the plan	Hold an Implementation Launch	
	Strengthen individual Employee Self-Leadership	
	Hold weekly Supervisor-Employee 1-1 Progress Reviews	
	Carry out Monthly Team Meetings, e.g., management & departmental	
	Hold Quarterly Review Meetings	
	Review and Update Your Strategic Plan annually	
7. Develop Human & Organizational Capacity	Assess Organizational High-Performance factors	
	Develop and implement an action plan to improve or enhance High Performance	
	Identify the employee competencies that the organization needs in next 5-10 years	
	Assess employees against the competencies	
	Develop and implement training and development plan to increase required competencies	
	Reassess organizational height performance	

Figure 48: 7 Steps Checklist to Create Your Future

Caution: you do not do everything on the checklist in the first year, or by the second year.

Implementing the 7-Step Creating Results Strategic Management process will help you more fully realize extraordinary results and higher employee engagement and performance.

Why I Wrote This Book

Hearing the Haida story of how the world was in darkness and the Raven brought the sun back to the sky, which is why we have sunlight today, reminded me of the ancient truth that without vision, we perish as we are in the dark!

The process I have described in the book helps people bring to light their inner vision about what they want to create. The Creating Results 7-steps outline envisioning and realizing your desired future and results.

This book is for you if...

- you are not satisfied with the status quo, it provides you with a proven and effective process to seize this moment in history to create a blueprint for self-determination.
- you want a better way to bring about needed changes and results.
- you want a systematic process to realize your desired future.

Writing this book has not happened overnight - it is a culmination of 40 years of experience working with leaders and members, employees of communities, not-for-profit, businesses, and corporations organizations, including Indigenous nations and organizations.

My work began in the late 1960s with a global social movement learning and applying participative methodologies to transform communities and organizations. Since then, I have had the opportunity to learn and use many methods for transforming organizations and communities as a volunteer and in professional roles working with diverse clients, ranging from Fortune 500 corporations to privately owned firms and not for profits. Approximately half of my clients over the years have been Indigenous organizations. I have acquired, applied, and adapted these methodologies to positively affect and create the desired changes in organizations and communities. Through these experiences, I have developed my own best practices for planning and implementation to help organizations continually evolve and transform.

The Creating Results Seven-Steps and best practices outlined in this book has helped diverse organizations achieve their desired results as indicated by the comments below:

"Your strategic planning and implementation expertise has helped us develop 3-year plans and to establish our one-year priorities. Establishing key success measures, key performance indicators, and targets helped us be results-focused and **achieve more extraordinary results consistently. Involving employees** *in the planning process helped them understand what goes into achieving the organization's mission and vision, to feel more connected with it, and* **their role and contribution to make it happen.**

You have instilled an inclusive planning and implementation process. It is a natural way of thinking and working and has helped us stay on track towards achieving our future and desired results". ˜ Nancy Stacey Director of Organizational Services of Kahnawake Economic Development

"Marcelene guided our leadership team in a breakthrough

alignment process to ensure excellent execution and achievement of our annual operating plan. Her tools, skills, and the alignment process helped us create focus on our priorities, high levels of teamwork, and confidence in our collective ability to create the successful future we want. Our ability to integrate and implement our plans is significantly improved over previous years and has had a direct impact on our bottom line." ~ John Holland, General Manager, Sara Lee Household & Body Care Division

Note: *This* division achieved its annual targets and won the President's award for the best performing division in its business category.

"The process you designed and facilitated with us has helped us work together more effectively as a team. The structured planning process helped us think about the organization's future and share and exchange our objectives. Through the process, we learned more about our organization, and our synergy has increased." ~ Albert Diamond, President of Air Creebec

"Your team proved that the impossible is possible. As you know, there was an overabundance of skepticism about the "restructuring and realignment project"; however, it turned out to be extremely successful. We are ahead of our implementation schedule by six months." ~ Peter Buddo Vice President of HR, Administration & Communication of Ericsson Canada.

With results like these, who wouldn't want to share the process and contribute to organizations that build our society!

Determine Your Future

This is not a "Strategic Planning for Dummies" book. It is for leaders who genuinely want a better future for their nation, community, or organization, and want to make a significant difference.

Neil Tichey, former CEO of GE articulated it well, "Those who do not determine their future, allow others to determine it for them."

I am committed to assisting leaders in determining the future of their organizations and communities. Nowhere is this needed more than in Indigenous nations and organizations worldwide.

Brian Patterson, President of USET, said, "I think it's time for Indian Country once again to dream the dream that our fathers and mothers dared to dream—the one that allowed our generation to advance on the path of sovereignty and self-determination."

In my work with Indigenous organizations, I have realized that for them to be sovereign nations and determine their futures again, it is necessary to have a plan to make it happen. They are not alone. All organizations need an inspiring vision and a future-focused, results-based plan to succeed. However, a plan is not enough! They also need a systematic process to implement the plan successfully.

I sincerely hope that the planning and implementation best practices and processes outlined in this book will provide you with a guide to help you succeed whether your goal is to:

- Improve the economic well-being of your citizens and your local and or regional economy
- Improve the quality of education
- Improve the quality of health care
- Continue to revitalize your culture
- Improve governance of your nation and
- Overall, improve the quality of life for your citizens.

I hope that the best practices will help you to:

- Improve and or enhance how your team, board or council, or management team works together to establish shared goals and achieve them
- Improve alignment within your organization
- Achieve more than previously thought possible
- Engage all your employees in creating a great future of which you are all proud.

Whatever outcomes you are seeking, my sincere hope is that by applying these best practices, you will be successful in achieving them.

Final Thoughts

When it comes to the future, there are three kinds
of people: those who let it happen, those who make
it happen, and those who wonder what happened.

John M. Richardson, Jr.

Many of the issues and challenges that nations, communities, or organizations face requiring longer-term thinking to bring about changes. Strategic planning allows management, a board of directors/ council, business leaders, and employees to consider possible alternatives, focus on the future direction for the organization, and develop the strategies and plans to achieve that future. Your strategic plan will provide a road map to your desired future for your organization and allow you to allocate resources strategically. In addition, your strategic plan will provide a framework for making decisions on an ongoing basis.

Over the past 40 years, I have witnessed firsthand how powerful and productive strategic planning can be. I've seen how it can bring companies and communities together and how it is pivotal in the success of many types of organizations. Developing and implementing a strategic plan allows goals to be achieved, results to be realized, and a reputation of excellence established.

I hope that the content of this book will provide you with a process and systematic approach for you to develop strategic and operational plans and successfully implement them, while building and maintaining a high-performance organization. Developing and implementing a plan requires a significant investment of time, new thinking, and change management strategies.

Over the years, it has been my privilege to work collaboratively with many leaders of Indigenous and non- Indigenous organizations and communities to develop their strategic and operational plans. I have seen the significant difference planning and implementation can make.

I hope you take advantage of my expertise and experience or another qualified strategic planner to help you develop and realize your vision for a healthy and vibrant community with a sustainable future.

I believe that the time is NOW for Indigenous people and nations to determine their desired future and create and successfully implement a road map to self-determine their future.

ROI for Strategic Planning

The real test of a Strategic Plan is whether it gets implemented and delivers the intended results.

Marcelene Anderson

I wish you much success in determining the future of your nation, community, and or organization to improve the lives of your citizens and employees. I am confident you can realize the future and results you and your nation desire and intend to achieve.

Why The Raven?

Around the world, the Raven is a recognized symbol of transformation and change.

- Sun, moon, and stars - Legends says the world was once in darkness. Raven's strategy brought the stars, the moon, and the sun to the sky to bring light to the world. Raven Strategic helps people discover and bring to light their vision for their future.
- Islands - Legends says Raven dropped small rocks into the ocean, creating islands, a place for people to rest. Raven Strategic planning process helps create a healthy environment for all people and creation.
- Salmon - Legends says Raven dropped little redfish eggs into moving waters running off the lands into the saltwater, bringing forth an abundance of fish for people. Raven Strategic planning process enables people to envision and realize abundance in their lives and communities.
- Trees and fruit. Legend says Raven spread berries and tree seeds over the land to bring forth all kinds of trees and food for people. Raven Strategic enables envisioning and realizing the sweet and good things of the land.
- Changing color of feathers – Legends say the Raven was white before flying through the smoke hole with the ball of light, turning its feathers black. Raven

Strategic recognizes that as change agents in the world, we too are changed in bringing change to the world.

- Feathers symbolize higher thought and outlook on life or a situation. Raven Strategic engages people in determining their higher-level purpose.
- Legends say the Norse god Odin had two ravens, Huggin and Muggin. Huggin, meaning thought, and Muggin, meaning memory. Raven Strategic helps people share their knowledge and wisdom.
- Raven Strategic helps people think together to create strategic solutions that make a profound difference.
- In Greek mythology, ravens are associated with Apollo, the god of prophecy. Raven Strategic process engages people to envision and proactively determine their future.

Like the Raven, each of us has the power to create and transform world.

I hope you will use your Raven power to transform your nation or community, organization, and transform your world and life.

About the Author:
Marcelene Anderson, MA, CMC

Marcelene grew up in the original homeland of the Dakota people, southern Minnesota. Living on the land inspired a sense of kinship with the Native Americans who had lived there for millenniums. Additionally, her father was a key person in her life, modeling respect for others, kindness, caring, and sharing. He inspired her to contribute to the lives of others. Over the years, she found a natural blending of this sense of kinship with Native Americans, love for Mother Earth, and passion for serving others.

After completing her degree in sociology, Marcelene began her career working with people in various capacities, ranging from being a caseworker, founding and directing early childhood learning programs, developing innovative health care education programs, designing training, and developing leadership and employee programs for a leading financial organization and becoming a management consultant. Concurrently, as a volunteer and national director for the forerunner to the Institute of Cultural Affairs, Marcelene had the opportunity to develop facilitation skills to work effectively and engage community groups, to work with people from all cultures, engaging them in planning their future and assisting them in developing solutions for their challenges.

As a result of her involvement in working with community groups and organizations to bring about transformation across North America and in communities across the world, Marcelene and her family relocated to Canada, beginning her work with Canada's First Nations and organizations.

A leading international consultancy hired Marcelene to be part of a specialized team to provide management consulting services to the Crees of Northern Quebec. This milestone marked the beginning of her ongoing commitment to serve Indigenous people and nations in the Americas and globally. She feels it is a privilege and a honor to walk on this path with Indigenous peoples and nations as they reclaim their identity, sovereignty, and self-determination.

As the founder and CEO of Raven Strategic Solutions, Marcelene has, over 40-years, worked with some 250 organizations of all types, from First Nations and Indigenous organizations to Fortune 500 corporations. She assists groups to determine their future direction, the results they want to achieve, develop and successfully implement plans to realize them into an integrated strategic management system.

To support the achievement of results, she also improves the effectiveness of organizations to achieve results over time. Marcelene has worked with senior corporate management,

Chiefs and councils, Boards of Directors, managers, and staff in the following areas: governance, strategy development, and implementation, and staff development. Additionally, she has worked in the following sectors: governance, housing, transportation, infrastructure, administration, economic development, health care, social services, and educational organizations.

Raven Strategic

After hearing one of the Haida legends of the Raven in the early nineties, Marcelene renamed her business, Raven. The legend says that long ago a powerful leader had taken and kept the sun hidden in a box in his house, leaving the world in darkness. Seeing that the world was in darkness and people were struggling, Raven created a strategy—by taking the form of the leader's grandson, Raven, used his powers to steal the sun. Returning to his Raven form, he flew the sun back into the sky. The proof is that we have sunshine today.

Before flying the sun back into the sky, another legend says, Raven had white feathers, and Raven's feathers turned black after flying through the smoke hole to take the sun back to the sky. As an agent of change, working with clients to assist them in improving their situations, Marcelene realizes that the process provides a mutual benefit as she has also been changed and has grown in helping clients realize their goals.

Legend says The Norse God Odin had two ravens, Huggin (translated as thought) and Muggin (translated as memory). Each day Odin sent out his messengers to fly around the world, Hugin, the messenger of thought, and Mugin, the messenger of memory. As a consultant, Marcelene helps people think together, share their knowledge and insights, and create the future they want.

The stories resonated with Marcelene as she had worked for many years helping organizations and groups to get in touch with, bring their vision to light, and create their desired future. She does not prescribe to her clients what their vision and their goals should be. Instead, her passion is assisting groups to focus, articulate what they want, organize into a cohesive dynamic and systematic plan that achieves results, and brings about planned changes on an ongoing basis.

She acts as an 'organizational midwife', assisting her clients in giving birth to their mission and vision, turning them into their desired results. The plan they create is theirs, with their hopes and dreams, a focused vision for their future, their goals/targets, strategies, and practical plans. As a midwife, she assists the organization in nurturing and realizing their objectives and developing the capability of their people.

Professional Background

Marcelene is a former partner of the Haines Centre for Strategic Management and was a Principal and a Senior Management Consultant with KPMG. She is a Certified Management Consultant (CMC), the highest professional standard in management consulting, recognized worldwide. She has a Gold Level Certificate in Strategic Management from the Haines Strategic Management Centre.

She has provided Change Management and Training Services to a wide range of corporate and public organizations. Over a ten-year period, Marcelene worked with community leaders on a volunteer basis across the United States and internationally to develop and implement methodologies to transform communities.

She has a Master of Human Systems Intervention from Concordia University in Montreal, Quebec, and a Bachelor of Sociology and Psychology Degree from Minnesota State University, Mankato, Minnesota. She also obtained a McGill University Certificate for completing the Executive Development Program.

Marcelene is a member of the Canadian Association of Management Consultants. In addition, she is a member of the New Management Network, a peer group of senior consultants who operate as a virtual organization. She is a member of the Native Canadian Centre of Toronto. She is a Board of Director of Ecologos, a not for profit organization, dedicated to preserving the reverence for water and water and environmental protection, and a volunteer at the Royal Ontario Museum.

She shares with you this quotation:

"This is the true joy in life, being used for a purpose recognized by yourself as a mighty one. I am of the opinion that my life belongs to the whole community, and as I live, it is my privilege—my privilege to do for it whatever I can. I want to be thoroughly used up when I die, for the harder I work, the more I love. I rejoice in life for its own sake.

Life is no brief candle to me; it is a sort of splendid torch, which I've got a hold of for the moment, and I want to make it burn as brightly as possible before handing it on to future generations".
George Bernard Shaw, Man and Superman, Epistle Dedicatory

How to Reach Us

No matter where you are on the journey to develop and successfully implement a strategic plan for your organization and become a high performance organization, Marcelene Anderson can help you to create the future you desire and deserve.

For more information about how Marcelene can help you or your organization, please visit www.ravenstrategic.com.

There you will find information on:

- The Strategic Management System, including the Strategic Management process to create a roadmap to your desired future, the systematic process to achieve results day to day, and change management services to realize transformation.
- Services to build and sustain a high performance organization.
- Programs and services to develop human capacity to increase performance and productivity.

To connect with Marcelene and her team, simply fire off an email to info@ravenstrategic.com and someone will get back to you within a day.

Figures

References

Assembly of First Nations | Dismantling the Doctrine of Discovery | January 2018.

Wendy Becker and Vanessa Freeman, *Going from Global Trends to Corporate Strategy*. The McKinsey Quarterly, McKinsey & Company 2006 Number 3.

James C. Collins and Jerry I. Porras, *Built to Last*. Harper Business, a Division of Harper-Collins Publishers. New York. 1997.

Collins, James and Porras, Jerry, *Built to Last–Successful Habits Of Visionary Companies*. Harper Collins. New York. 2002.

Jim Collins, *Good to Great. Why some companies make the leap ... and others don't*, London: Random House. 2001.

Stephen R. Covey, The *Seven Habits of Highly Effective People*. Simon & Schuster. New York. May 1984.

Viktor E. Frankl, *Man's Search for Meaning* (Boston: Houghton Mifflin, 2000.

Richard Beckhard and R. Harris, *Organizational Transitions: Managing Complex Change* (2nd Ed.) New York: The Free Press. 1987.

Emerging Trends Affecting Public Service and the Public Service Employment Act. Public Service Commission Canada. 2009.

Daniel Goleman, *Leadership That Gets Results.* Harvard Business Review. March–April 2000.

Robert S. Kaplan and David P. Norton, with Edward A. Barrows, Jr., *Developing the Strategy: Vision, Value Gaps, and Analysis.* Balanced Scorecard Report. Harvard Business School Publishing Corporation. January–February 2008.

Stephen Haines, *Systems Thinking Approach to Strategic Management.* CRC Press LLC. Boca Raton Florida. 2000.

James. Kouves, Barry Z. Posner. *The Leader Challenge,* Jossey-Bass. San Francisco. 2007.

Richard Leider, *The Power of Purpose.* Berrett-Koehler Publishers Inc., San Francisco. 2004.

Arthur Manuel and Grand Chief Ron Derrickson. Between the Lines, Unsettling Canada A National Wake-Up Call, p 10

Robert J. Miller, The Doctrine of Discovery: The International Law of Colonialism

McKinsey & Company, *Creating More Value With Corporate Strategy,* McKinsey Global Survey Results. 2011.

C. Chet Miller and Laura B. Cardinal, *Strategic Planning and Firm Performance: A Synthesis of More Than Two Decades of*

Research. Academy of Management Journal. 1994, Vol. 37, No. 6. 1649-1665.

Robert J. Miller, *The Doctrine of Discovery: The International Law of Colonialism*

John Nesbitt, *Mind Set! Reset Your Thinking and See the Future.* Harper Collins. New York. 2006.

Tom Peters and R. Waterman, *In Search Of Excellence*, New York: Warner Books. 1982.

Marco Schreurs, *What is High Performance Organization* Center for Organizational Performance.

Peter Senge, *The Fifth Discipline.* Doubleday Dell Publishing Group Inc. New York. 1990.

R. Brian Stanfield, *The Workshop Book*, New Society Publishers, [Paperback], 2009

Jim Stewart, *8 Things That Hinder Growth*, ProfitPATH Blog, September 11th, 2012.

Jesse Stoner, Don Carew, Eunice Parisiarew, and Fay Kanadrian. *High Performing Organization Profile.* The Ken Blanchard Companies. 2005.

Andre de Wal, Ph.D., *The Characteristics of High Performance Organizations.* In A. Neely, M. Kennerley and A. Walters (Ed.), Performance Measurement and Management: Public and Private, Cranfield School of Management. 2006.

Andre de Wal, Ph.D., *Working on High Performance in the U.K:*

An overview of current research and practical application. Center for Organizational Performance. www.hpo.com 2010.

Thomas J. Watson Jr., *A Business and Its Beliefs*, New York: McGraw Hill, 1963.

Marvin Weisbord, *Future Search: Getting Whole System Into the Room.* Berrett-Koehler Publishers. 2010.

Robert Wright, Stolen Continents: The "New World" Through Indian Eyes p4. (1999)

Printed in the United States
by Baker & Taylor Publisher Services